Country Roads of

WISCONSIN

Drives, Day Trips, and Weekend Excursions

Second Edition

Don Davenport

COUNTRY ROADS PRESS

NTC/Contemporary Publishing Group

Library of Congress Cataloging-in-Publication Data

Davenport, Don.
    Country roads of Wisconsin : drives, day trips, and weekend
excursions / Don Davenport.—2nd ed.
        p.   cm.—(Country roads)
    Includes index.
    ISBN 0-658-00243-0
    1. Wisconsin Guidebooks.   2. Automobile travel—Wisconsin
Guidebooks.   3. Rural roads—Wisconsin Guidebooks.   I. Title.
II. Series.
    F579.3.D36   2000
    917.7504'43—dc21   99-40606
                                                                                CIP

Cover design and interior design by Nick Panos
Cover illustration copyright © Todd L. W. Doney
Interior site illustrations and map copyright © Leslie Faust
Interior spot illustrations copyright © Barbara Kelley
Picture research by Jill Birschbach
Typeset by Varda Graphics, Inc.

Published by Country Roads Press
A division of NTC/Contemporary Publishing Group, Inc.
4255 West Touhy Avenue, Lincolnwood (Chicago), Illinois 60712-1975 U.S.A.
Copyright © 2000, 1996 by Don Davenport
Printed in the United States of America
International Standard Book Number: 0-658-00243-0
00 01 02 03 04 05 ML 20 19 18 17 16 15 14 13 12 11 10 9 8 7 6 5 4 3 2 1

For Mary Jo and Bitsy—treasured traveling companions

Wisconsin Country Roads
(Figures correspond with chapter numbers.)

Contents

Introduction

I grew up in a family where a drive in the country was an important part of life. Then, I saw them simply as fun, but looking back, I can see they served many purposes—not the least of which were entertainment in the days before television and escape from the heat when home air-conditioning was a luxury still in the future.

Sometimes we drove only as far as downtown, a matter of a few blocks, to watch the evening train from Chicago arrive. Other jaunts took us off to explore the countryside or to visit relatives in nearby towns (usually fun, but not always—it depended on the relatives). On those occasions, we often took a different route home. Just because.

I learned about geography on those family drives, and about history, and I developed a sense of the land and a lifelong appreciation for round barns and cut-limestone houses. I also stored away sights, sounds, and smells for future reference. To this day, the scent of new-mown hay on a warm June night or the pungent aroma of wood smoke or burning autumn leaves sends me soaring back across the decades, to specific drives and times and places.

Early on, I developed an itch to go—somewhere, anywhere—and I learned that getting there is half the fun. These days, the dog and I usually take a different route home from the post office after we've picked up the morning mail. Just because. And sometimes, when the call is too strong to ignore, we sneak off for a midweek drive, justifying the time away from work with a walk in the country and the exercise that both of us need (so that's why you were late with the story!). And it's a rare weekend that my wife and I don't pack up the dog and go for a drive. Somewhere. Anywhere. Just because. Sadly, there are no longer trains from Chicago to be met.

I have been exploring the back roads and byways of Wisconsin for more years than I care to admit, so when the opportunity to write this book came along, I jumped at the chance.

Driving Wisconsin's country roads in the guise of research gave me good reason to return to favorite places, as well as to travel to some that I'd never been to, places that, for one reason or another, just never got visited. Yet one of the most eye-opening experiences I had was traveling along a country road that I had driven literally thousands of times before. Dictating into a tape recorder as I went, I saw things that I'd never noticed (or perhaps failed to pay attention to) on all those drives. And I was shocked to realize that "improvements" made over time—eliminating a curve here, straightening things a bit there—had changed the road until only a very few miles of it remained as it was in my youth.

Wisconsin is a land of great diversity and, I think, great beauty. Much of the Badger landscape was carved by the Ice Age glacier millennia ago. The Kettle Moraine, in the southeast corner of the state, is internationally famous for its glacial landscape, but the vast, mile-thick ice sheet left its mark almost everywhere in the state, save for the far southwestern corner.

Wisconsin has 250 miles of Mississippi River shoreline, making up about half of its western border. The Lake Superior coast, on the north, is 156 miles long. Lake Michigan, to the east, has a shoreline of just over 400 miles. Only along the southern border with Illinois do rivers or lakes not come into play in determining the state's boundaries.

In between are nearly 110,000 miles of excellent roads, including some 12,000 miles of state highways, 20,000 miles of county roads, and 75,000 or so miles of local roads. So many roads, so little time.

The dozen tours outlined in this book are intended as day or weekend excursions. But Wisconsin is a fairly large state: It may take a day's drive simply to get to the starting point of some of these country roads.

Most of the driving tours begin in the south and work their way to northern areas of the state. That's the natural flow of traffic in Wisconsin, dictated in part by geography and in part by tourism patterns (hello, Chicago, and welcome!). Along the way, we'll visit places that are well known, including Door County, the Apostle Islands, Devil's Lake State Park, the House on the Rock. And we'll visit places not so well known, such as the world's largest block letter "M," the National Freshwater Fishing Hall of Fame, Amnicon Falls State Park, the Merrimac Ferry.

You'll need a road map as you begin your excursions. A detailed atlas or gazetteer can be helpful if you intend to wander off the beaten path. By all means, do so. There are 72 counties in Wisconsin, each with hundreds of miles of country roads that beg to be explored.

The Wisconsin Department of Tourism (P.O. Box 7976, Madison, WI 53707) offers a wealth of free material on virtually every facet of Wisconsin travel, from cheese-factory tours, watercraft rental, bed-and-breakfasts, camping, golf, fishing, skiing, snowmobiling, and hiking, to calendars of events and much more. Call 800-432-8747, 24 hours a day, seven days a week, or 800-372-2737, from Monday through Friday, 8:00 A.M. to 4:30 P.M. The local tourism offices and chambers of commerce listed at the end of each chapter are also good resources.

It is said (sometimes jokingly) that Wisconsin has but two seasons: winter and road construction. Be that as it may, you can get a statewide update of detours, road closures, traffic inconveniences, or winter road conditions by calling 414-785-7140 (Milwaukee), 608-246-7580 (Madison), or 800-ROAD-WIS (Wisconsin and neighboring states).

Information on state parks and forests is available from the Wisconsin Department of Tourism; call 800-432-8747. You can reserve a campsite by calling 888-947-2757. An admission fee is required to enter state parks.

Many of the attractions mentioned in this book are open seasonally; others are open only on certain days of the week. I suggest that you call ahead to any of those that you especially want to visit.

With that, it's time to choose a country road, fasten your seat belt, and get going! Bring your camera and lots of film. And don't forget to buy some cheese while you're there.

1

Swiss Cheese and Norwegian Trolls

Getting there: From Chicago (approximately 135 miles), take I-90 northwest to Rockford, and follow U.S. Route 20 west for 30 miles to Freeport. Go north on State Highway 26 to the state border, where the road becomes State Highway 69.

From Milwaukee (approximately 110 miles), take I-43 southwest to Beloit, and follow State Highway 81 west to Monroe.

Highlights: Charming ethnic towns to explore; Monroe and the Cheese Hall of Fame; New Glarus, plus the Swiss Historical Village Museum and Chalet of the Golden Fleece Museum; Mt. Horeb, Little Norway, Cave of the Mounds, and Blue Mound State Park. The driving distance is approximately 50 miles. Allow one day, minimum.

On any Friday afternoon, between April and October, State Highway 69, which runs for 45 miles from the Wisconsin–Illinois border to the suburbs of the state capital of Madison, bustles with northbound traffic. Cars bearing Illinois license plates with bicycles atop their roofs

I

head for the Sugar River and Military Ridge State Trails. Motor homes and RVs are bound for south-central state parks. Autos with trailers and boats seek out the lakes surrounding Madison or beyond.

Late on Sunday afternoon (morning, if the weekend has been rainy or especially cool), the traffic heads southward. But the pace is slower, the excitement of the weekend getaway dwindling. With another workweek looming on the horizon, the boaters, campers, and bicyclists prolong the day, stopping to buy a pound of the cheese for which the region is famous or to simply take time to enjoy the scenery.

Heading northward from the Wisconsin–Illinois border, neat farms with red barns and tall, silver-topped silos set among rolling hills mark the road's approach to Monroe, the county seat of Green County and "Swiss Cheese Capital of the USA." Cheese making, introduced by Swiss immigrants, began around 1845. Today, Green County factories produce some 55 million pounds of cheese each year. There's Swiss, of course, known as "Green County Gold," along with Cheddar, Colby, Monterey Jack, Muenster, and others. Some factories offer tours. Visit the Cheese Hall of Fame, in a former railroad depot along State Highway 69 at the southwest edge of the city, for information on cheese-factory tours and exhibits about the county's cheese industry.

It follows then that Cheese Days (held the third weekend in September on even-numbered years) is Monroe's big event, celebrating the county's ethnic and cheese-making heritage with Old World music, dancing, and a parade that draws more than 100,000 visitors.

Downtown Monroe surrounds a square dominated by the century-old, Romanesque-style Green County Courthouse, with its 120-foot-high clock tower (133 steps to the top to repair the clock). It's a beauty, so bring your camera. Sample Green County Gold at Baumgartner's Cheese Store and Tavern, on the west side of the square. Although nothing fancy, it's nationally famous as a spot to enjoy a cold local brew and a Swiss on rye.

Two old churches within easy walking distance of the square now house a museum and a gallery. One block north, the Green County Historical Museum, located in a former Universalist Church (circa 1861) that stored wheat and wool for the Union Army during the Civil War, has exhibits of tools and other items used by early settlers. A furnished, late-1880s schoolhouse stands nearby (both open Saturday and Sunday afternoons, Memorial Day through September). Two blocks west of the square on Eleventh Street is the Monroe Arts Center, housed in the Gothic-style Old Methodist Church, designed in 1869 by Milwaukee architect E. Townsend Mix. Listed on the National Register of Historic Places, it's now a cultural center featuring art exhibits, drama, and special events.

For more local flavor, food, and spirits, try the Suisse Haus, a block south of the square (great homemade soups). On the north edge of town is the Peppercorn Cafe. With a huge stone fireplace in the dining room, it's a cozy spot to enjoy fine dining. Chocolate Temptation, on the square, offers taste treats, such as hand-dipped chocolates and pumpkin cheesecake.

Heading northward from Monroe, State Highway 69 climbs, swoops downhill, and climbs again, all the while winding through a patchwork of rolling, rocky hills and oak woodlots lining a broad, meandering valley. More farms here and prize herds of Brown Swiss and Holstein cows to produce the milk that goes into all that cheese. Contour farming of corn, oats, and hay gives the land a flowing, sculptured look.

Sixteen miles north of Monroe, the road slides downhill into the valley of the Little Sugar River and the village of New Glarus (population 1,900), founded in 1845 by immigrants from Glarus, Switzerland. After 150 years, the Swiss–German dialect is still spoken, and village architecture retains a 19th-century Old World flavor. Newer additions—banks, motels, grocery stores, restaurants, office buildings, even the veterinary clinic—are done up in a Swiss mountain–chalet style, sporting emblems of the Swiss cantons and flower boxes filled with red and white flowers. One bank features an outdoor, 18-bell glockenspiel that marks the hours and provides bell concerts during the day. Nearby, the Swiss United Church of Christ, on its front lawn, has a monument to the pioneer settlers, and there's a four-faced clock in its tall steeple. Take a moment to enjoy the working floral clock (Sixth Avenue at State Highway 69), and allow some time for exploring the nooks-and-crannies shops that offer imported Swiss items; European pastries; and recordings by local bands, singers, and yodelers.

Restaurants serve Old World delicacies year-round. The New Glarus Hotel, established in 1853 (live polka bands and dancing on Friday and Saturday nights), and the Glarner Stube (STEW-ba) are popular with tourists. Both are located on First Street.

The annual Wilhelm Tell Festival, held each Labor Day weekend, features Swiss singing, dancing, yodeling, and other entertainment and centers around Friedrich von Schiller's epic drama of Swiss independence, *Wilhelm Tell*. There's a cast of hundreds, including horses, cattle, and goats (it's held outdoors), with performances in both English and German.

To learn the story of Swiss immigration and settlement, visit the Swiss Historical Village Museum, a complex of a dozen original and reconstructed buildings perched on a hilltop overlooking the village. The Chalet of the Golden Fleece Museum, built as a private residence in 1937, has an eclectic collection that ranges from Swiss wood carvings to a jeweled watch once owned by King Louis XVI of France. Both museums are open May through October.

If outdoor pursuits are your pleasure, New Glarus is the northern terminus of the Sugar River State Trail, a hiking/biking trail that follows a former railroad right-of-way for 23 miles to Brodhead, passing through a covered bridge along the way. Trail headquarters, in an old railroad depot downtown, provides shuttle service and bike rental.

New Glarus Woods State Park, a mile south of town on State Highway 69, has camping, hiking, and picnic facilities. It's easy to reach via the paved biking/walking path from the village. The park entrance road, County NN, follows an old Winnebago Indian trail. The first band of Swiss colonists followed this road to their new home in August 1845.

If you're in town between late August and early November, visit the Swiss Valley Orchard (three miles north on County O) for apples, apple pastries, homemade cider, and other tasty treats.

For a glimpse of New Glarus as it was before the village and tourism discovered each other, have a cold local brew and a sandwich at Puempel's Olde Tavern, downtown near the floral clock. A New Glarus landmark since 1893 (the "Olde" is a recent affectation), the tavern has a long, narrow taproom with a tin ceiling and hand-painted alpine murals done by a traveling artist in 1912.

Should you wish to linger, the Chalet Landhaus Inn offers Swiss architecture and modern comforts.

Heading northward, our country road continues to climb. Four miles north of New Glarus, at the top of a long hill, say good-bye to State Highway 69 and turn west on State Highway 92. The Swiss chalets disappear as the highway drops into another broad valley, and the names on farm mailboxes take on a Norwegian flavor.

Just north of the crossroads hamlet of Mt. Vernon, the valley narrows, the hills move closer, and the road curves and winds as it climbs ever upward. Not a drive for someone in a hurry, but why hurry? "Sweet Corn for Sale" signs pop up in farmhouse yards in August, and onetime cheese factories turned into dwellings (easily recognizable by their long, narrow shapes and glass block windows) dot the way.

Winding up one final hill, State Highway 92 ends in Mt. Horeb. With its wide, tree-lined streets and rambling Victorian homes, there's little to set this Norwegian community aside from other Wisconsin towns of its size (population 4,500).

Except for the trolls.

You know, trolls—those none-too-bright, slightly seedy characters in the Norse folktales.

Turn left onto the Trollway (Main Street) at the end of State Highway 92, and keep an eye peeled for these whimsical creatures. Carved from wood, and usually found standing atop an old tree stump, most are the work of local artist Mike Feeney.

You'll find many ways to contribute to the local economy here. Gift shops featuring imported Scandinavian delights, quilts, and Christmas items, as well as several large antiques malls, are all downtown.

On Main Street, check out the zany Mt. Horeb Mustard Museum (more than 2,000 different mustards in the collection), and learn more than you'll ever want to know about the "spice of nations."

When it's time for a break, follow the signs to Steward County Park, one mile north of town, where a pretty, man-made lake offers a delightful spot for a picnic.

Back in town, head west on Main Street, which becomes County ID, a ridge-top road that provides spectacular views of the Wisconsin River valley on the northern horizon and of a broad, flat prairie to the south. The gravel path beside the road is the Military Ridge State Trail, a biking/hiking trail that runs for 39 miles between Verona and Dodgeville. Here, the trail follows the route of the Old Military Road, built in 1838 to connect Fort Crawford on the Mississippi River with Fort Winnebago on the Wisconsin River and Fort Howard at Green Bay.

More trolls along the way—five keep watch over traffic from a farmyard along the north side of the road. Three miles west of town, turn north on County JG and wind down through the woods to Little Norway, a pioneer Norwegian farmstead founded in 1856. A dozen log buildings of authentic Norse architecture—carved dragon heads on the roofs ward off evil spirits—are filled with antiques, tools, and exquisite examples of traditional Norwegian arts and crafts. The farmstead's showpiece is a *stavekirke*, or stave church, built in 12th-century style. Used as the Norwegian Pavilion at Chicago's 1893 Columbian Exposition, it was moved here in 1935. Its treasures include an original manuscript written in 1873 by famed Norwegian composer Edvard Grieg.

Bid farewell to Little Norway's trolls, backtrack to County ID, and turn west (right). The grayish-blue hills ahead are Blue Mounds. A landmark since pioneer times and the highest point in southern Wisconsin (1,716 feet above sea level), the mounds mark the eastern edge of southwestern Wisconsin's lead-mining region. Perched at the top is Blue Mound State Park, with great scenic views, picnic and playground areas, hiking trails, campsites, and the only swimming pool in a Wisconsin state park.

At County F, you can make a short detour north to Cave of the Mounds, located on a farm established in 1828. The cave is noted for the variety, color, and delicacy of its rock formations. Easy walking guided tours take about an hour.

From here, you can follow County F west into the tiny village of Blue Mounds and take Park Road north one mile to Blue Mound State Park. Or follow County F north one mile to Brigham County Park, with more camping, picnic areas, and scenic views. When it's time to head home, pick up U.S. Route

18/151, which parallels County ID a quarter mile to the south. It's a four-lane highway all the way through Madison (25 miles east), where you can connect with I-94 to Milwaukee or I-90 to Chicago.

For More Information

Monroe Area Chamber of Commerce: 608-325-7648

Baumgartner's Cheese Store and Tavern (Monroe): 608-325-6157

Monroe Arts Center: 608-325-5700

Suisse Haus (Monroe): 608-325-3220

Peppercorn Cafe (Monroe): 608-329-2233

Chocolate Temptation (Monroe): 608-328-2462

New Glarus Tourism and Chamber of Commerce: 608-527-2095 or 800-527-6838

New Glarus Hotel: 608-527-5244 or 800-727-9477

Glarner Stube (New Glarus): 608-527-2216

Swiss Historical Village Museum (New Glarus): 608-527-2317

Chalet of the Golden Fleece Museum (New Glarus): 608-527-2614

Sugar River State Trail (New Glarus): 608-527-2334

New Glarus Woods State Park: 608-527-2335

Swiss Valley Orchard (New Glarus): 608-527-5355

Puempel's Olde Tavern (New Glarus): 608-527-2045

Chalet Landhaus Inn (New Glarus): 608-527-5234 or
  800-944-1716

Mt. Horeb Area Chamber of Commerce: 608-437-5914 or
  888-765-5929

Mt. Horeb Mustard Museum: 608-437-3986

Military Ridge State Trail: 800-432-8747

Little Norway (Blue Mounds): 608-437-8211

Cave of the Mounds (Blue Mounds): 608-437-3038

Blue Mound State Park: 608-437-5711

2

Wisconsin River Adventures

Getting there: From Chicago (approximately 185 miles), take I-90 northwest to State Highway 33 (about 35 miles north of Madison). Follow State Highway 33 west for 13 miles to Baraboo.

From Milwaukee (approximately 115 miles), take I-94 west to Madison, and follow I-90/94 northwest to State Highway 33, then head west to Baraboo.

Highlights: Wisconsin River scenery and small towns to explore; Baraboo area with the Circus World Museum, Mid-Continent Railway Museum, Devil's Lake State Park, and Merrimac Ferry; Spring Green with the Frank Lloyd Wright estate and American Players Theater. The driving distance is approximately 55 miles. Allow a weekend.

This Wisconsin River adventure begins at the northern terminus of State Highway 113, in Baraboo, where on May 19, 1884, five brothers named Ringling gave the first performance of their "Great Double Shows, Circus and Caravan."
The circus that was to become "The Greatest Show on Earth" had its winter quarters in Baraboo from 1884 to 1918,

when it was merged with the Barnum & Bailey Circus and moved east to Connecticut. Today, the State Historical Society's Circus World Museum occupies this hallowed ground along the Baraboo River, keeping alive the traditions of the circus with live performances under a 2,000-seat Big Top; parades; demonstrations; clowns; cotton candy; and the world's largest collection of restored, antique circus wagons.

"Ladieeees and gentlemeeeen . . . childreeeen of all ages!" Spangles, spotlights, and a wonderfully tinny circus band. Easy to spend the day here. Then take a short stroll along Water Street where some of the old circus buildings now house businesses and light industry; many have placards indicating their original purpose.

Circus money built some of the beautiful Victorian mansions you'll find scattered around Baraboo. One such is the Gollmar Guest House, which offers bed-and-breakfast accommodations in an elegant Victorian home. The Sauk County Historical Museum is housed in a 14-room mansion built in 1906; exhibits of Native American artifacts, pioneer relics, and Civil War memorabilia will acquaint you with Baraboo's history before the circus came to town.

Downtown, on the courthouse square, is the magnificent Al Ringling Theatre. Built by the eldest Ringling brother as a movie and vaudeville house, it's still in operation and little changed since opening night in 1915. Tours are available.

Now, we've two side trips to take, even before setting out on State Highway 113. Cranes or trains, take your pick.

Cranes? Five and a half miles north of Baraboo on U.S. Route 12 and a mile east on Shady Lane Road, you'll find the International Crane Foundation, a center for the study, propagation, and preservation of endangered crane species. Guided or self-guided tours are available from May through October.

Trains? Head west on State Highway 136 through rolling farmlands to County PF, then south to the village of North Freedom (total eight miles) and the Mid-Continent Railway

Museum. Steam-train rides through a countryside dotted with neat farms and cornfields recall the golden era of railroads. There are museum exhibits, an original 19th-century depot, and rolling stock on display. The museum is open spring through autumn.

Back in Baraboo, head south on State Highway 113. Crossing the Baraboo River, the road winds and climbs into a range of lush, wooded hills known as the Baraboo Bluffs. The bluffs are among the most ancient rock outcrops on the planet, formed, geologists believe, more than a billion years ago.

At the top of the bluffs, take County DL west (right) two miles to the north entrance of Devil's Lake State Park, or follow State Highway 113 down the bluff for a mile or so to South Lake Road, the park's south entrance. With 500-foot bluffs surrounding a sparkling, spring-fed lake, Devil's Lake is a place of exquisite, rugged beauty—there's really nothing quite like it elsewhere in Wisconsin.

Fishing, swimming, windsurfing, snorkeling, hiking and nature trails, scenic picnic areas, and three campgrounds give visitors lots to do. A good thing, since about two million people come to visit each year.

Continue south and east on State Highway 113 to the village of Merrimac, on the shores of Lake Wisconsin (created by a dam on the Wisconsin River). Lots of weekend bungalows along the lake here and mom-and-pop-housekeeping cottage resorts serving mainly fisherfolk.

But no bridge. The Merrimac Ferry, established in 1844, provides the State Highway 113 link across the Wisconsin River. Listed on the National Register of Historic Places, the ferry is a free service of the Wisconsin Department of Transportation. The *Colsac II*, named after the two counties the ferry serves—Columbia and Sauk—operates 24 hours a day from approximately April 1 to December 1, depending on ice conditions, and carries more than 200,000 vehicles each season. Its capacity is 12 autos—less, of course, if there are motor coaches or trucks aboard. At peak times, summer weekends and autumn-color season, the wait can be long. Go ahead! Treat yourself to something sweet at one of the concession stands near the ferry landing, and settle in for some great people watching. Once aboard, it's okay to step out of the car after the ferry is loaded. But don't dawdle. The one-mile crossing takes a little under 10 minutes.

A wayside rest area by the landing on the south bank of the river is one of the best places to photograph the ferry, especially in the afternoon light. If you're staying anywhere close by, give serious consideration to returning for a night crossing. It can be a romantic, albeit short, moonlight cruise.

After leaving the ferry, turn right on State Highway 188, and follow it southwest on a winding journey through a landscape of rolling farmland, wooded hills, and ridges. Two miles east of Prairie du Sac (12 miles from the ferry landing), State Highway 188 joins State Highway 60. Approaching Prairie du Sac, on the Wisconsin River, State Highway 188 turns south and shortly thereafter ends; State Highway 60 crosses the bridge into town.

A mile south on State Highway 188, high on a hillside overlooking the Wisconsin, is the Wollersheim Winery. One of the oldest vineyards in America, the winery was founded in the 1840s by Count Augustin Haraszthy, a Hungarian immigrant who is considered the father of viticulture in California. Tours and tastings are available year-round.

Prairie du Sac, on the west bank of the river, hosts the Wisconsin State Cow-Chip Throw each Labor Day weekend. The last of 26 hydroelectric dams that make the 430-mile Wisconsin "the hardest working river in the nation" is located two miles above town. From here, the Wisconsin flows free for 93 miles to the Mississippi. Bald eagles are a common sight in winter, flying along the bluffs, sitting in trees along the river, or fishing the open waters below the dam.

Pick up State Highway 78 in Prairie du Sac, and follow it south through town into adjacent Sauk City, a major jumping-off point for canoe trips on the Lower Wisconsin. Stay on State Highway 78 as it crosses the Wisconsin River and turns south (right) immediately after the bridge.

A mile or so farther along, just beyond the intersection with County Y, where the road hugs the base of the river bluffs, a force of some 1,000 soldiers fought a pitched battle with a small band of Sauk and Fox Indians during the brief Black Hawk War of 1832. In a skirmish now called the Battle of Wisconsin Heights, the Sauk chieftain Black Hawk and some 50 warriors fought a holding action on the bluff top during a driving rainstorm, allowing hundreds of old men, women, and children to escape across the river just beyond. Describing the Indians' bravery and military skill, U.S. Army Lieutenant Jefferson Davis (who may or may not have been there) wrote: "Had it been performed by white men, it would have been immortalized as one of the most splendid achievements in military history."

The road now pulls away from the Wisconsin, winding past wooded ridges and around gumdrop-shaped hills, skirting the sand hollows and cattail swamps that dot the river's floodplain. After 12 miles, State Highway 78 intersects with U.S. Route 14. Turn west (right) onto U.S. Route 14, and follow it west through the village of Mazomanie. The Wisconsin has also turned west and now lies a mile and a half to the north.

A mile beyond Mazomanie, a wayside rest area marks the site of Dover, a once sizable village founded in the 1840s by members of the British Temperance and Emigration Society. All that remains today is a tiny pioneer cemetery where the headstones all bear the name Culver. Following the Civil War, local farm boy John Appleby invented the knotter on the grain binder, grasping the idea as he watched the regular movement of his mother's hands while she knitted. He successfully tested his invention in 1867, in a wheat field just east of the wayside.

Continuing westward, U.S. Route 14 hurries through the village of Arena. A quarter mile south of town (follow Reimann Road) is the Chapel in the Pines. Set at the end of a sandy lane, in a grove of red pine and scrub oak trees, the small log chapel is open to all; it is never locked.

Continuing west from Arena, U.S. Route 14 cuts through the Wisconsin's broad, flat floodplain, bounded north and south by high rounded bluffs. The sandy river bottomlands are ideal for growing fruit and vegetables. From midsummer to late autumn, roadside produce markets sell sweet corn, melons, pumpkins, squash, and other delicious homegrown goodies.

Nine miles farther along is Spring Green, a farming community known worldwide as the home of the architect Frank Lloyd Wright.

Turn south (left) on County C just before the Wisconsin River bridge, a mile or so east of town. Along this three-mile stretch of wooded road between U.S. Route 14 and State Highway 23, you'll find Tower Hill State Park, the American Players Theater, and the Frank Lloyd Wright Visitors Center.

Tower Hill State Park marks the site of the former village of Helena (1830–1857). A reconstruction of a shot tower used to manufacture lead shot during the 1840s stands on a bluff overlooking the Wisconsin. The park offers hiking trails, a small campground, picnic facilities, and a canoe landing. The old Helena Cemetery is at the top of a wooded hill across from the park entrance.

The renowned American Players Theater, located just south of Tower Hill and a half mile east on Golf Course Road, offers Shakespeare and other classics under the stars in a beautiful outdoor amphitheater from mid-June into October, with bug spray furnished free. Pre-show special events include "Skippeth Out of Work Early" (Thursday nights) and Friday-night fish boils. There's a picnic area on the grounds. Make time to take in a performance; they're wonderful.

Across the road from American Players Theater, The Springs Golf Club Resort offers several reasons to linger: championship golf courses, fine dining, beautiful scenery, and luxurious accommodations.

The Frank Lloyd Wright Visitors Center, overlooking the Wisconsin River at the junction of County C and State Highway 23, was formerly the Spring Green, a restaurant designed by Wright in 1953. It includes a cafe, a bookstore, and an exhibit area. It is the starting place for a wide range of Wright estate tours, including walking tours of Wright's home (reservations required).

Wright built the home he called Taliesin ("Shining Brow" in the Welsh language) in 1911, on a hillside overlooking the river valley three miles south of Spring Green. It was his principal home and office for nearly 50 years. Here, the noted architect produced some of his most famous designs, including Falling Water (Pennsylvania), the Johnson Wax Buildings (Wisconsin), and the Guggenheim Museum (New York).

The name Taliesin refers both to Wright's home and the 600-acre estate, which contains other buildings he designed: Hillside Home School (1902), Midway Farm (1930s and 1940s), Tan-y-deri House (1907), and Romeo and Juliet Windmill (1897). The estate is a National Historic Landmark.

Just opposite the entrance to Taliesin (State Highway 23 and County T) is Unity Chapel, designed in 1886 by Chicago architect Joseph Silsbee. Several members of Wright's family are buried in the chapel cemetery, including his mother, his sister, and five of his children. A stone bearing the name Anne Baxter Klee honors the memory of Wright's granddaughter, the actress Anne Baxter, who is buried elsewhere.

Wright was buried here upon his death in 1959. In 1985, under the terms of his third wife's will, the architect's body

Frank Lloyd Wright's home, Taliesin, near Spring Green

was exhumed and moved to Arizona. Wright's original gravestone now marks an empty grave.

Nearby, Spring Green (population 1,283) has a number of buildings that were designed by associates or students of Wright. Downtown, two buildings of the M&I Bank on Jefferson Street, the outdoor garden at the Post House restaurant, also on Jefferson Street, and St. John's Catholic Church on South Washington Street were designed by longtime Wright associate William Wesley Peters. At the north edge of the village, along U.S. Route 14, the Prairie House Motel, Round Barn Lodge, and Usonian Inn were designed by former Wright students.

The river valley's lush, wooded beauty and Wright's ongoing influence have drawn many artists and craftspeople to the Spring Green area. You'll find the works of several regional artists showcased at Jura Silverman Gallery on South Washington Street.

When the weekend is over, U.S. Route 14 will take you east to Madison (40 miles) and the interstates leading to Chicago or Milwaukee.

For More Information

Baraboo Area Chamber of Commerce: 608-356-8333 or
  800-227-2266

Circus World Museum (Baraboo): 608-356-0800 (24-hour
  information)

Gollmar Guest House (Baraboo): 608-356-9432

Sauk County Historical Museum (Baraboo): 608-356-1001

Al Ringling Theatre (Baraboo): 608-356-8864

International Crane Foundation (Baraboo): 608-356-9462

Mid-Continent Railway Museum (North Freedom):
608-522-4261 or 800-935-1385

Devil's Lake State Park: 608-356-8301

Wollersheim Winery (Prairie du Sac): 800-847-9463

Spring Green Chamber of Commerce: 608-588-2042 or
800-588-2042

Tower Hill State Park: 608-588-2116

American Players Theater (Spring Green): 608-588-7401 or
608-588-2361 (box office)

The Springs Golf Club Resort (Spring Green): 800-822-7774

Frank Lloyd Wright Visitors Center (Spring Green): 608-588-7900

Jura Silverman Gallery (Spring Green): 608-588-7049

3

Getting the
Lead Out

Getting there: From Chicago (approximately 190 miles), take I-90 northwest to Madison, and follow U.S. Route 14 west to Spring Green (40 miles).

From Milwaukee (approximately 125 miles), take I-94 west to Madison, and follow U.S. Route 14 west to Spring Green.

Highlights: Historic mining towns and remnants of Wisconsin's lead region; the House on the Rock; Dodgeville and Governor Dodge State Park; Mineral Point with Pendarvis State Historic Site, arts and crafts, and early Wisconsin architecture; Belmont and the First Capitol Historic Site; Platteville and the Mining Museum. The approximate driving distance is 75 miles. Allow a day and a half.

This tour begins in Spring Green, which is discussed in Chapter 2. Heading south from Spring Green, State Highway 23 provides another glimpse of Frank Lloyd Wright's work. Standing among the wooded hills four miles south of town is the Wyoming Valley School, which Wright designed in 1956. After 30 years of service (1958–1988), the two-classroom school was closed and is now privately owned.

This country road now does some serious climbing as it winds to the top of a high, razor-backed ridge. Here and there along the way, half hidden among the trees, stunning country homes show Wright's strong influence.

At the top of the ridge, and down a lane marked by Oriental sculpture, is the famous House on the Rock. Begun more than 50 years ago as a weekend retreat, the house was built atop a 60-foot chimney of rock. It now contains 14 rooms, with pools of running water, massive fireplaces, waterfalls, multistory bookcases, and an Infinity Room that extends more than 200 feet into free space, providing views that turn the knees to jelly.

The complex has been expanded over time to include a Circus Building with miniature circuses; a Doll Building with more than 250 dollhouses; the Music of Yesterday Museum with automated, animated musical machines; and, my favorite, a giant carousel with more than 20,000 lights and 269 figures, but no horses.

Wait, there's even more than that. An Organ Building with three of the world's largest theater organ consoles, Streets of Yesterday with a re-created 19th-century Main Street, Heritage of the Sea Building with hundreds of ship models and a 200-foot-
long sculpture of an octopus, and several specialty rooms. Hundreds of thousands of items and artifacts are displayed. And there are shops and restaurants. Touristy? Yes. But chances are you've never seen anything quite like it. You'll walk a mile or so to take it all in.

Back on the highway, down off the ridge, through a valley, up another hill. Barns and silver-capped silos decorate the ridge tops, cows cling to the wooded hillsides. (Is it true that grazing on the steep hillsides makes their legs on one side shorter than on the other?)

The flat-topped, grayish-blue hills growing on the southeastern horizon are the Blue Mounds, a landmark since pioneer times and the highest point in southern Wisconsin (see Chapter 1).

Three miles north of Dodgeville is 5,029-acre Governor Dodge State Park. Known for its rugged wind- and water-sculpted sandstone bluffs, the park is popular with campers; the first visitors were nomadic hunters who camped here more than 8,000 years ago. Except for the entrance sign, you could drive by and never know the park was here—Governor Dodge doesn't reveal its true beauty until you drive down into its valleys. There are two man-made lakes, if you're ready for a dip, and some lovely spots for a picnic.

Dodgeville, settled by lead miners in the late 1820s, was named for Henry Dodge, a miner, militiaman, and politician who became territorial Wisconsin's first governor. At the north edge of town, a tall tree fashioned from steel wagon wheels and a huge, four-engined Stratocruiser airliner mark the Don Q Inn, famous in the Midwest for its specialty rooms (tours of the fantasy suites are offered on weekends). Across the road is The Thym's, long a favorite area supper club.

Dodgeville is the seat of Iowa County. The state's oldest active courthouse, in continuous use since 1861, stands in the center of town. Few traces of the mining days remain here, save for some mine tailings (piles of waste rock from the mines) along the south side of U.S. Route 18/151 at the east edge of town.

Heading southwest from Dodgeville, State Highway 23 is joined by U.S. Route 151 in a winding, seven-mile, hilltop jaunt to Mineral Point.

Lots of early Wisconsin history is here, and there are some beautiful old buildings. Pick up brochures, pamphlets, and a guide (modest cost) outlining a walking/driving tour of architectural highlights at the Mineral Point Tour Center, in the stone cottage by the water tower on U.S. Route 151. If it's closed, try the Chamber of Commerce office on High Street.

Sprawled across hillsides that descend into a narrow valley, Mineral Point dates from 1827, when prospectors began seeking lead. The discovery of large deposits of nearly pure lead in 1828 brought a stampede of miners and settlers, setting off the nation's first big mineral boom. Mineral Point (lead was called mineral, the big strike was made on a point of land, hence, Mineral Point) soon became the metropolis of southwestern Wisconsin's burgeoning lead region. By 1834, more than half of the 5,400 people living in what is now Wisconsin lived in and around Mineral Point.

On July 4, 1836, newly created Wisconsin Territory— carved from Michigan Territory, which was headed for statehood—was formally inaugurated at Mineral Point, and Henry Dodge was officially sworn in as the first territorial governor. Thousands flocked into the rough, crude, and muddy mining town (one of the more complimentary contemporary descriptions called it "humble and unpretending in appearance") to celebrate.

At the peak of production, in the late 1840s, the lead region, which included a corner of northwest Illinois, produced nearly 85 percent of the world's supply of lead. Lead mining in Wisconsin slowly declined after 1850, although there were production jumps during the Civil War, World War I, and World War II. Following the Civil War, zinc mining became nearly as important as lead mining, but it faded after World War I. The last mines in southwest Wisconsin were closed in the 1970s.

In the 1830s and early 1840s, Cornish miners from Cornwall, England, began to arrive here in substantial numbers. It is their strong heritage, with the pasties and saffron cakes, stone cottages and folktales, that gives Mineral Point its charm. In 1971, it became the first Wisconsin city listed on the National Register of Historic Places.

Don't miss Shake Rag Street, in the valley at the bottom of town, where miners' wives shook a rag to summon their men home from mines in the nearby hills. There are several lovely old stone cottages here, as well as Pendarvis State Historic Site, a Cornish miners' colony named for an estate in Cornwall. Costumed guides tell tales of life on Shake Rag as they lead you through six restored, furnished cottages and row houses built in the 1840s. Mind your head passing through the doorways; although tough as the rock they blasted in the mines, the men of Cornwall were not noted for their height.

A walking trail beginning at the Pendarvis parking lot climbs a hill to the site of the old Merry Christmas Mine. The hillside is dotted with "badger holes" (tiny pit mines) from long ago. Early miners lived in these holes like badgers, earning Wisconsin its nickname of the "Badger State."

Mineral Point supports a thriving art community, with several galleries and shops. Look along High Street, Commerce Street, and Jail Alley to find many antique and gift shops.

Take note of the statue of a dog mounted on the building at 215 High Street. Cast of zinc, the dog was originally used to promote a 19th-century department store that stood here, following a British custom that identified stores by statues of animals, in the same way that cigar stores were identified by carved figures of Native Americans. Its origins are vague, but the dog has looked down on some 125 years of Mineral Point history.

Sample a pasty (PASS-tee) before you leave. A convenience food that miners took to work, pasties were a kind of meat pot pie that contained whatever meat and vegetables were available at the time, baked into a crust sturdy enough to be dropped down a mine shaft without breaking. (Strong teeth, those miners.) Today's pasties contain beef, potatoes, and onions baked in a tender and flaky crust and are a stick-to-the-ribs meal in themselves. Most local restaurants serve them.

If you wish to linger, Mineral Point has several bed-and-breakfasts.

Pick up U.S. Route 151 at the water tower and follow it southwest along a ridge top to Belmont (13 miles). At Belmont, turn right on County G, and follow it north three miles to First Capitol Historic Site.

One of Henry Dodge's first acts as territorial governor was to name Belmont, which existed mainly on paper, to be the capital of Wisconsin Territory. In 1836, this included all of present-day Wisconsin, Iowa, Minnesota, and the Dakotas as far west as the Missouri River.

With the region's sparse timber supplies reserved for the lead smelters, a frame Council House (capitol) and Supreme Court Building were hurriedly pre-cut at Pittsburgh and shipped down the Ohio River, up the Mississippi and Fever Rivers to Galena, Illinois, then hauled overland to Belmont and assembled.

The first territorial legislature convened here on October 24, 1836. In a stormy session that lasted 46 days, the legislators designated Madison as the permanent capital. After the legislature adjourned, Belmont died aborning. Present-day Belmont (on U.S. Route 151) was established in the 1860s with the coming of the railroad.

Despite checkered careers as barns, homes, and what-have-you, both the original Council House and the Supreme Court buildings survive, standing along the road in a parklike setting shaded by maples and surrounded by farm fields. The Council House contains reproductions of 19th-century tables, chairs, desks, and a few original furnishings. The Supreme Court building has exhibits about territorial government and history.

From First Capitol Historic Site, follow County B and continue west past cornfields and dairy farms to the intersection of West Mound Road (four miles). A hundred feet or so north on West Mound is the world's largest block letter "M," built in

1937 by students of the Wisconsin Mining
School in nearby Platteville (today the
College of Engineering at the University
of Wisconsin–Platteville). Constructed of
large whitewashed stones set into the side
of a hill, the "M" measures 241 feet high
by 214 feet wide. On a clear day, you can
see it from more than 20 miles away; it's most impressive
when seen from a distance. There's a picnic table here, and, if
you're feeling energetic, steps to the top of the hill.

Continue west on County B to Platteville, a lead-mining
town dating from 1827 and named for the plattes, or ingots,
into which the smelted lead was formed for shipping. The road
leads straight to the Mining Museum, where dioramas, artifacts, models, and photos trace the development of lead and
zinc mining in the region. There were thousands of lead mines
and hundreds of deep-shaft zinc mines in southwestern
Wisconsin and northwestern Illinois—the exact number is
unknown. Three separate lead mines underlie the hill on which
the museum stands; 16 zinc mines are located within a one-
mile radius.

The museum highlight is a guided tour of the Bevans
Mine, an 1845 lead mine 50 feet below ground. Put on your
hard hat (furnished), and follow the 90 concrete steps leading
down into the mine (and—gasp—back up). While the mine
has been enlarged for tour purposes, you can see just
how small the lead mines were in the side drifts, or tunnels,
which are mere crawl spaces. The tour includes a visit to an
aboveground hoist house of a zinc mine (replicated) and a
bone-jarring ride around the grounds on a mine train, with
authentic ore cars pulled by a small, gasoline-powered mine
locomotive. Admission to the Mining Museum includes a tour
of the adjacent Rollo Jamison Museum, with a vast and eclectic collection of arrowheads, appliances, tools, and items from
the early 1900s.

The Chicago Bears of the National Football League hold their summer training camp on the campus of the University of Wisconsin–Platteville. Should you be in town mid-July to mid-August, stop by. Admission is free. You can stand or sit on a hillside (blankets and lawn chairs welcome) overlooking the practice fields and watch the current crop of Bears perform. Even Green Bay Packer fans show up to check out the competition.

In summer, the University of Wisconsin–Platteville hosts a celebrated, monthlong Wisconsin Shakespeare Festival.

Leaving Platteville, follow State Highway 80 south past contoured cornfields through Cuba City to State Highway 11 (12 miles), and turn east to Benton, another old lead-mining community. Swindler's Ridge Museum, on Main Street, features mining and military exhibits and an old general store.

The cemetery at St. Patrick's Church, at the east edge of town, is the final resting place of Father Samuel Mazzuchelli, a Dominican priest and missionary who ministered to the needs of the people of the lead region from 1835 to 1864. Known to the Irish miners as "Father Matthew Kelly," Mazzuchelli addressed the opening session of the territorial legislature at Belmont. A noted amateur architect, he designed and built as many as 20 churches and secular buildings in Wisconsin, Illinois, and Iowa, including St. Patrick's. The church and the restored church rectory, built in 1864, are open to visitors.

From St. Patrick's, take County J south for three miles to County W, then head east two miles to New Diggings, a hardscrabble mining hamlet near the Illinois border. Turn right on County I, and follow it up the hill to St. Augustine's Church (on the left), which Mazzuchelli built in 1844. Weathered and rickety with age, the wood-frame church stands in tribute to the tireless priest who devoted much of his life to serving the lead region.

Back on County W, continue east. Here and there are scattered traces of the mines—piles of rock debris, sand-choked hillsides and valleys, concrete slabs or stone foundations from ore-processing plants. Here stood the Mulcahy Mine, the Blackstone, the Calumet and Hecla, and dozens more unnamed, now long gone. A mountain-sized pile of debris at the intersection with County O marks the site of one of the region's largest zinc mines.

Turn north (left) on County O and follow it into Shullsburg. Downtown are stone, brick, and tin-fronted buildings and streets named Faith, Hope, Charity, and Judgement. Badger Park, at the south edge of town, is the site of the Badger Mine and Museum, a small lead mine that's open for tours in summer.

From Shullsburg, State Highway 11 east leads to the southern terminus of State Highway 23, where you can backtrack through Mineral Point and Dodgeville to Spring Green. Or continue east on State Highway 11 to Monroe (25 miles), where State Highway 69 leads south into Illinois and connections to I-90 east.

For More Information

House on the Rock (Spring Green): 608-935-3639

Governor Dodge State Park: 608-935-2315

Don Q Inn (Dodgeville): 608-935-2321

The Thym's (Dodgeville): 608-935-3344

Mineral Point Chamber of Commerce: 608-987-3201 or 888-764-6894

Pendarvis State Historic Site (Mineral Point): 608-987-2122

First Capitol Historic Site (Belmont): 608-987-2122

Platteville Chamber of Commerce: 608-348-8888

Mining Museum and Rollo Jamison Museum (Platteville): 608-348-3301

Wisconsin Shakespeare Festival Box Office (Platteville): 608-342-1298

Swindler's Ridge Museum (Benton): 608-759-5182

Badger Mine and Museum (Shullsburg): 608-965-4860

4

The Great River Road, Southern Segment

Getting there: From Chicago (approximately 185 miles), take I-90 northwest to Rockford, and follow U.S. Route 20 west for 90 miles to East Dubuque, Illinois. The Wisconsin–Illinois border and the beginning of Wisconsin's Great River Road lie at the north edge of the city.

From Milwaukee (approximately 165 miles), take I-43 southwest to Beloit, and then continue by following State Highway 81 west to Monroe. From Monroe, follow State Highway 11 west to State Highway 35.

From Minneapolis–St. Paul (approximately 160 miles), follow U.S. Route 61 south to La Crosse, Wisconsin, and State Highway 35.

Highlights: Cassville, the Cassville Car Ferry, Stonefield Historic Site, and Nelson Dewey State Park; Prairie du Chien, Wyalusing State Park, and Villa Louis; spectacular river scenery and 19th-century architecture along the entire drive. The driving distance is approximately 125 miles. Allow a weekend.

Wisconsin's segment of the Great River Road runs along the east bank of the Mississippi River for a distance of nearly 250 miles. Not especially well known outside the immediate area, it may well be one of the Midwest's last "undiscovered" scenic drives, following a narrow shelf of land between some of the highest bluffs found on the river and the Big Muddy itself. Along the way, you'll discover fascinating, hard-edged river towns, where history hangs in the air like haze on an autumn afternoon.

This tour covers the southern half of Wisconsin's Great River Road, from the Wisconsin–Illinois border north to La Crosse. The northern portion of the route is covered in Chapter 5.

We begin in the far southwestern corner of Wisconsin. For the first 10 miles of the journey, State Highway 35 is four lane, joined by U.S. Route 61/151 and bustling with traffic heading in and out of the tristate area of Wisconsin, Illinois, and Iowa. Pick up maps, brochures, and information about area attractions at the Wisconsin Travel Information Center, located a mile north of the Wisconsin–Illinois border on a cloverleaf at the intersection of State Highway 35, State Highway 11, and U.S. Route 61/151. But mind your p's and q's, or you'll end up on the U.S. Route 61/151 bridge headed for Iowa.

The four-lane road ends at Dickeyville, home of the Dickeyville Grotto, one of the more unusual attractions along the way. Father Matthias Wernerus built the grotto on the grounds of Holy Ghost Church between 1925 and 1930, using stones, colored glass, and bits of this-and-that gathered from around the world to construct several religious and patriotic shrines. Working out the designs in his head as he went along, Father Wernerus pieced each together like a giant jigsaw puzzle. Beautiful floral gardens surround the shrines.

From Dickeyville, the Great River Road follows State Highway 35/U.S. Route 61 northwest, crossing the Platte River as it winds past steep, wooded ridges and slides through valleys, climbing a ridge to the adjacent villages of Tennyson and Potosi (the "Catfish Capital of Wisconsin"). Approaching Tennyson, the white letter "M" you see in the distance off to the east is the world's largest block "M" (see Chapter 3).

Originally called Dutch Hollow, Tennyson took root during the early 19th-century lead-mining days and remained a mining town until the 1960s, when the last mine was closed. Tradition says that John Wilkes Booth, the actor who assassinated President Abraham Lincoln, once performed here. To see the older section of the village, turn east (right) onto County O and follow it down the hill for a block or two.

Return to State Highway 35/U.S. Route 61, and follow the Great River Road as it turns south on State Highway 133, sliding downhill into Potosi, which claims the longest main street without an intersection in the world (three miles). An 1830s mining town once known as Snake Hollow, Potosi (a Spanish word meaning "mineral wealth") was once a bustling port on the upper Mississippi. But in 1846, Potosi's harbor silted in and the river abandoned it, leaving the community high and dry.

Our country road slithers down Snake Hollow through the village and past some fascinating old limestone buildings to the St. John Lead Mine (about two-thirds of the way down the hollow). Here, in 1690, French trader Nicolas Perrot was shown Snake Cave, where local Indians were mining lead. Cornish miners began reworking the old Indian diggings in 1827, expanding the natural cave into the St. John mine, which operated until 1870. The mine is listed on the National Register of Historic Places. Guided tours are available from May through October; you can also rent canoes for use on the nearby Grant and Big Platte Rivers. Tour maps outlining a 12-mile driving tour of early historic sites in the region are available here and at other local businesses.

Finally, at the bottom of the hollow, the Great River Road provides the first, tantalizing glimpse of the Mississippi.

A scene along the Great River Road

There's a lovely spot to picnic or to stretch your legs at the Grant River Recreation Area, an Army Corps of Engineers park and campground overlooking the river two miles south of Potosi. Turn south (left) on Park Lane at the foot of the hollow and follow the signs.

For most of its length, the Great River Road closely parallels the high-speed tracks of the Burlington Northern Santa Fe Railway. At the time this was written, more than 30 fast freight trains traveled the line each day. For many of us, trains are but a fading memory—remember to use caution whenever crossing the tracks.

Back on State Highway 133 and heading northwest, the Great River Road runs along the base of high river bluffs for a spell. Sliding past Dog Tail Road and across the Grant River, it swings to the east and climbs to a ridge dotted by small farms and woodlots, with the river's west-bank bluffs (Iowa) two or three miles distant. Near Cassville, the road returns to the Mississippi.

You'll be seeing double, even triple, if you happen to visit Cassville on the third weekend in July. The annual Twin-O-Rama celebration draws hundreds of sets of twins and triplets from across the country as well as thousands of spectators. Large numbers of bald eagles take up residence in winter, feeding in the open waters below the dam at nearby Guttenberg, Iowa.

Cassville made a bid to become the territorial capital in 1836 but came up short. The former Denniston House, a three-story brick hotel built by local promoters as an enticement, still stands along the riverfront. A ferry began operating here that same year and ran for more than a century. The village re-established the service in 1988, and the Cassville Car Ferry carries passengers and autos across the Mississippi to Millville, Iowa (May through October). It's the only river crossing between Dubuque, Iowa, and Prairie du Chien, Wisconsin, a distance of 62 miles.

At the northwest edge of town, on County VV, Stonefield, the State Historical Society's museum of agricultural history and village life, re-creates an 1890s rural Wisconsin hamlet. Stroll the town square and visit with costumed merchants and tradesmen at the shops and businesses or take a horse-drawn carriage ride across a covered bridge to a 1901 farmstead. The State Agricultural Museum exhibits farm implements, machinery, models, tools, and other items that trace the development of Wisconsin agriculture from the mid-19th century into the 1920s.

Across the road is the reconstructed homestead of Nelson Dewey, the state's first governor. Although the home burned in 1873, the reconstruction has some original furnishings and several original outbuildings from the estate. Guided tours are available.

Next door is 750-acre Nelson Dewey State Park. Follow the winding park road through the woods to the top of the river bluffs, where there are ancient Hopewell Indian mounds, picnic areas, and spectacular views of the Mississippi, the first of many along the Great River Road.

Continue north on County VV through hill-and-hollow farm country to County A (about 11 miles), passing Good-Nuff Hollow Road, Muddy Hollow Lane, and Rock School Road along the way. Turn northwest (left) on County A and follow it past Dry Hollow Road into Bagley, on the river. From Bagley, follow County X north along the river to the village of Wyalusing, which has a public swimming beach on the Mississippi. Two miles farther north is Wyalusing State Park.

Established in 1917, Wyalusing (why-a-LOOS-ing, an Indian word meaning "home of the warrior") stands atop 300-foot bluffs at the confluence of the Wisconsin and Mississippi Rivers. It was here, in 1673, that Father Jacques Marquette and Louis Jolliet discovered the upper Mississippi. Recording the event in his journal, Marquette wrote: "After we arrived at the mouth of our river (Wisconsin), we safely entered the Mississippi on the 17th of June with a joy that I cannot express."

Point Lookout, near the main parking area, offers terrific views of the bluffs on the Iowa shore, the nearby city of Prairie du Chien, and the junction of the two rivers far below. Every 60 seconds, 15.8 million gallons of Mississippi River water flow past this point. Hike Sentinel Ridge Trail to see ancient Indian mounds and more river scenery. The park also offers scenic campgrounds, picnic areas, and a nature center. During the spring and autumn migrations, vast numbers of ducks, geese, hawks, and eagles pass this way.

Leaving the park, follow County X northwest to County C and turn left, winding down a wooded ridge to State Highway 35/U.S. Route 18. Turn left again and follow State Highway 35/U.S. Route 18 across the Wisconsin River to Prairie du Chien.

Prairie du Chien (French for "prairie of the dog") stands on a broad, flat plain between rocky bluffs and the Mississippi. Wisconsin's second oldest city, after Green Bay, it was a flourishing fur-trading center a full century before the American Revolution, attracting Indians, traders, and settlers to an annual spring and autumn rendezvous on the prairie beneath the bluffs.

A minor skirmish in the War of 1812 was fought here in 1814. In 1832, Prairie du Chien's frontier military outpost of Fort Crawford was the setting for a romance filled with passion, drama, and tragedy.

Soon after his arrival at Fort Crawford, Lieutenant Jefferson Davis, U.S. Army, fell in love with Sarah Knox Taylor, the daughter of Colonel Zachary Taylor, his commanding officer.

They began an ardent courtship, and Davis asked Colonel Taylor for Sarah's hand in marriage. Taylor's "no" was emphatic. The lovers became secretly engaged and continued the clandestine relationship.

In the spring of 1833, Davis was transferred to St. Louis. He resigned from the army two years later, and Sarah decided to marry him without her father's permission. They were wed in Louisville, Kentucky, on June 17, 1835.

During a honeymoon in Louisiana, both were stricken with malaria. Sarah Knox Taylor died on September 15, less than three months after her marriage to Jefferson Davis. She was 21 years old.

Zachary Taylor was elected president of the United States in 1848. He died in 1850, serving little more than a year in office.

After Sarah's death, Jefferson Davis took up the life of a Mississippi planter. In 1845, at age 37, he married 18-year-old Varina Howell and went into politics. He served as U.S. Secretary of War (1853–1857) during the administration of Franklin Pierce and became the U.S. senator from Mississippi in 1857. He resigned that office in 1861, on the day that Mississippi seceded from the Union. Returning home, Davis was named president of the Confederacy.

Stop at the Wisconsin Travel Information Center (U.S. Route 18 at the Mississippi River bridge) for information about Prairie du Chien and environs.

The city's premier attraction is the Villa Louis, a genteel Victorian mansion standing atop an ancient Indian mound beside the Mississippi. Designed by Milwaukee architect E. Townsend Mix, the cream-colored brick mansion was built in 1870 by the family of Hercules Dousman, an early fur trader and agent for John Jacob Astor's American Fur Company. Its furnishings include one of the nation's finest collections of decorative arts—china, glass, artwork, books, and silver that were used by the Dousman family from 1843 to 1913. Museum exhibits in the former carriage house depict the early history of Prairie du Chien. The old Astor Fur Warehouse, on the grounds, has exhibits on the early fur trade. Costumed guides lead tours of the mansion and grounds (May through October).

Four military posts stood on what became the estate grounds, including Fort Shelby, where that battle in the War of 1812 was fought, and the first of two Fort Crawfords built at Prairie du Chien. A replica of a fort blockhouse and foundation, outlines of original fort buildings, can be seen on the mansion grounds.

A stone's throw away along the river is Lawler Park, where the first steamboat called in 1823. The famous paddle-wheel riverboats, *Mississippi Queen* and *Delta Queen*, and new *American Queen* stop here in summer, continuing the long tradition.

The second Fort Crawford, where Jefferson Davis was stationed, stood back from the river about a mile south of the first fort. The Prairie du Chien Museum at Fort Crawford, housed in the restored fort hospital, features exhibits on local history, including 19th-century medicine.

Close by is a small U.S. military cemetery where fort soldiers and their wives are buried.

Heading north from Prairie du Chien on State Highway 35, the Great River Road hugs the Mississippi shore, climbing along a shelf that broadens and narrows as high, rocky river bluffs move close, then wander away. Where space permits, cottages with neat lawns nestle at the foot of the bluffs. Elsewhere, there is room for little more than the highway and the railroad tracks. In places, signs warn of the possibility of fallen rocks, so take heed.

Twelve miles north of Prairie du Chien, at River Mile 647.9, is Lock and Dam No. 9, one of 29 locks and dams on the upper Mississippi that make possible commercial navigation between Minneapolis and St. Louis. Each dam in the system creates a miles-long lake, called a pool, to maintain a minimum of nine feet of water in the main river channel. The locks raise upward-bound river traffic to the level of the upstream pool and lower the downward-bound traffic to the level of the downstream pool. Observation platforms provide close views of the fascinating locking process.

Continue north on State Highway 35, where herons and egrets keep watch over traffic from bottomland sloughs and swamps, gulls and terns fly low above the river, and turkey vultures ride the bluff-top thermals. Tiny towns, long and narrow, timeworn around the edges, slide by at intervals of 8 to

10 miles. Each seems to have a Front, River, or Water Street along the Mississippi. "Smoked Fish," "Fresh Fish," and "Night Crawlers for Sale" signs are plentiful.

At Lynxville, the larger-than-life figures of the community's Christmas crèche look down from the bluffs year-round. During the logging era, when logs were floated down Wisconsin's rivers to the Mississippi and southward, the largest raft of logs on the river was assembled here. More than 1,500 feet long, it contained two and a quarter million board feet of lumber.

The hamlet of Ferryville, originally called Humble Bush, opted for a name change when a ferry was established in the mid-19th century (now long gone). The cheese factory at the north end of town produces Muenster, Cheddar, and Colby, among other cheeses, and has a retail shop.

Eight miles farther north is De Soto, named for the Spanish explorer who discovered the Mississippi in 1541. The river is island choked here, with more trees than water, or so it seems from the Great River Road.

On August 1 and 2, 1832, the bloody final engagement in the Black Hawk War was fought along the river and bluff tops between De Soto and Victory, four miles to the north. The Battle of Bad Axe, named after a river that flows nearby, concluded a series of skirmishes with Sauk and Fox Indians that began in Illinois three months earlier. Several historical markers detailing local Native American history and the war's end are found along this section of the Great River Road.

Just up the river is Blackhawk Park, an Army Corps of Engineers' park offering riverside campsites, picnic areas, a swimming beach, and boat-launching facilities.

Opposite the hamlet of Victory (don't blink), the forested bluffs on the Mississippi's west bank come under new management as Iowa ends and Minnesota begins. A mile or so north of town, the Great River Road scurries across the Bad

Axe. It seems a small, muddy stream to have gained so much historical notoriety.

On November 11, 1940, Armistice Day, this stretch of the river witnessed another great tragedy. On a day that began more like June than November, hundreds of lightly clad duck hunters made their way into the Mississippi bottomlands of west-central Wisconsin, northeast Iowa, and southeast Minnesota. That afternoon, a savage autumn storm roared unannounced out of the Great Plains, hammered into a raging blizzard by blinding snows and winds of 65 miles per hour. When it was over, some 50 hunters were dead. More than a half century later, the event remains etched in local memory.

The village of Genoa, nestled in a riverside valley north of Victory, was called Bad Axe until Italian immigrants renamed it in 1868 to honor Christopher Columbus. Lock and Dam No. 8 (River Mile 679.2) is located at the south edge of town.

North of Genoa, there's a short stretch of river with few islands. Here, the village of Stoddard was inducted into the fraternity of river towns in 1937, when the pool created by the construction of Lock and Dam No. 8 put the river at its doorstep.

Not far above Stoddard, the Great River Road takes on the hurly-burly look of the approach to a city—more signs, more traffic, more sprawl. U.S. Route 14/61 swings in from the east and suddenly we're in La Crosse, Wisconsin's largest city on the Mississippi.

We're also at the end of the southern segment of the Great River Road. But there's more to come.

For More Information

Wisconsin Travel Information Center (Kieler): 608-748-4484

Dickeyville Grotto: 608-568-3119

St. John Lead mine (Potosi): 608-763-2121

Grant River Recreation Area (Potosi): 608-763-2140

Cassville Department of Tourism: 608-725-5855 or
888-675-3330

Cassville Car Ferry: 608-725-5180 (24-hour recording)

Stonefield Historic Site (Cassville): 608-725-5210

Nelson Dewey State Park: 608-725-5374

Wyalusing State Park: 608-996-2261

Prairie du Chien Chamber of Commerce and Tourism Council:
608-326-8555 or 800-732-1673

Wisconsin Travel Information Center (Prairie du Chien):
608-326-2241

Villa Louis (Prairie du Chien): 608-326-2721

Prairie du Chien Museum: 608-326-6960

Blackhawk Park (De Soto): 608-648-3314

5

The Great River Road, Northern Segment

Getting there: From Chicago (approximately 275 miles), follow I-90 northwest to La Crosse.

From Milwaukee (approximately 205 miles), take I-94 west to Madison, and follow I-90 northwest to La Crosse.

From Minneapolis–St. Paul (approximately 150 miles), follow U.S. Route 61 southeast to La Crosse.

Highlights: Picturesque river towns with locks and dams; La Crosse, Granddad Bluff, Hixon House, and Swarthout Museum; Trempealeau, Perrot State Park; Fountain City, Merrick State Park; Alma, Buena Vista Park; Pepin, Laura Ingalls Wilder history. The driving distance is approximately 125 miles. Allow a weekend.

Western Wisconsin's largest city, La Crosse (population 51,000), is set on a wide prairie beneath the bluffs at the junction of the La Crosse, Black, and Mississippi Rivers. Eighteenth-century French traders named the region after they saw Indians playing a ball game similar to the game of lacrosse. Today, the National Football League's New Orleans Saints hold their summer training camp on the prairie (mid-July to mid-August) at the University of Wisconsin–La Crosse. Practices are open to the public.

At the turn of this century, a half dozen breweries called the city home. Only G. Heileman remains in operation (tours available year-round). The La Crosse County Historical Society maintains three museums that peek into the area's past: the Hixon House, an opulent mid-19th-century Italianate-style mansion; the Swarthout Museum (in the main library), with changing exhibits of local history; and the Riverside Museum, which tells the story of the river's importance to the region's growth and development.

The city's best-known attraction, Granddad Bluff (two miles east on Main Street; follow the signs to the top), towers more than 500 feet above the Mississippi. There's a bird's-eye view of the city from the top; on a clear day, you can see Wisconsin, Iowa, and Minnesota.

La Crosse is the crossroads of two important hiking/biking trails—the Great River State Trail (24 miles), which runs north along the Mississippi to Trempealeau, and the La Crosse River State Trail (21 miles), which runs east to Sparta, where it connects with the nationally famous Elroy–Sparta State Trail. Together, the three trails offer more than 75 miles of hiking and biking through some of western Wisconsin's finest scenery.

When it's time for dinner, Piggy's on Front Street, overlooking the river, is famous for pork and beef. The Freight House offers fine dining in a former railroad freight house that's listed as a National Historic Site.

Heading north from La Crosse, State Highway 35 hurries past suburban Onalaska, Midway, and Holmen before it turns west, scurrying across the swampy Van Loon Wildlife Area and into Trempealeau (pronounced TREMP-a-low).

Founded in 1851, the village was named after Trempealeau Mountain, a 385-foot rock outcrop in the Mississippi that early French traders called La Montagne Oui Trempe a l'Eau (the mountain whose foot is bathed by water). The mountain, a mile or so upriver, has been a navigation landmark for more than three centuries.

After fire destroyed the riverfront business district in 1888, the Trempealeau Hotel and five other surviving buildings were moved to form the nucleus of the present Main Street District, which is listed on the National Register of Historic Places. The hotel, established in 1871, is a neat old place with squeaky wooden floors and offers both dining and lodging.

Lock and Dam No. 6 lies at the end of Fremont Street, adjacent to the marina at the south edge of the village. An observation deck provides close views of lock operations.

Two miles northwest of the village, where the Mississippi and Trempealeau Rivers meet, you'll find Perrot State Park, one of those "undiscovered gems" often read about but rarely found. Named for fur trader Nicolas Perrot, who spent the winter of 1685 to 1686 here, the park has ancient Indian mounds and picnic areas along the river and soaring bluffs with stunning views of the river valley. A wooded family campground, a nature center, and hiking and cross-country ski trails are added attractions. The Great River State Trail runs along the north edge of the park.

Heading north from Trempealeau, State Highway 35 pulls away from the river for a short swing through flat farmland where roadside stands offer pumpkins, squash, melons, and other local produce in season. At Centerville, a crossroads hamlet, the Great River Road turns sharply west, crossing the Trempealeau River at the huge Trempealeau National Wildlife Refuge (5,600 acres), and swinging back to the Mississippi shore.

Here, the steep, rocky bluffs crowd close, and egrets and herons cast a wary eye from backwater ponds and sloughs. The road ambles past Lock and Dam No. 5A and into

Fountain City, a picturesque village where stone walls support terraced gardens and houses cling to the sides of the bluffs.

The river bluffs are called "hard heads" here—they're round at the top, with little or no vegetation. The tallest, 550-foot Eagle Bluff, is the highest point on the upper Mississippi. In April 1995, a 55-ton boulder fell from the bluffs and crashed into a house below, narrowly missing a resident (can you imagine the noise?). The house is now a local attraction called Rock in the House. The Army Corps of Engineers has a boatyard and maintenance depot in Fountain City, homeport for the dredge *Thompson*, which helps maintain the river's nine-foot-deep navigation channel.

Merrick State Park, two miles northwest of town, has hiking trails, picnic areas, and family campsites right beside the Mississippi. It's a wonderful spot for bird-watching, especially during the annual migrations.

The great river and the Great River Road drift apart northwest of Fountain City, and the hard heads meander away for a spell, then hurry back to snuggle close. Just beyond the village of Cochrane, with its feed mills and grain elevators, Huber Ridge takes shape, then Lizzy Pauls Pond. Minutes later, Alma comes into view.

Squeezed onto a narrow strip between the river and Twelve Mile Bluff, bustling Alma is only two streets wide— Main and Second—but it's seven miles long (it seems shorter). Much of the downtown district—an engrossing collection of 19th-century buildings with balconies and battlement ends; shops sporting tin-covered fronts; and classic, Greek Revival–style brick buildings—is listed on the National Register of Historic Places. Along Main Street, the Laue House Inn (1863), the Gallery House Bed and Breakfast (1861), and the Sherman House "farmer's hotel" (1866) present a good argument for staying the night.

Lock and Dam No. 4 is located in the heart of town, right beside Main Street. A pedestrian overpass above the Burlington Northern Santa Fe tracks leads to the observation area along the lock wall. For a high-speed thrill, stand atop the overpass as one of the fast freights thunders through town.

Don't miss Buena Vista Park, overlooking Alma from a bluff top 500 feet above the river (take County E east and up). From here, you can see the entire layout of Lock and Dam No. 4, with its long earthen dike reaching across to the Minnesota shore. You can also see far up and down the river valley. The view rates a 10, minimum.

Back on State Highway 35 and heading north, Rieck's Lake, at the mouth of the Buffalo River along the north edge of Alma, has picnic areas and a campground. Look for eagles in winter, Canada geese and tundra swans in autumn, egrets and herons in spring and summer.

Onward. The Great River Road climbs a bit to look down on the river, but still snuggles close to the ever-present bluffs. The village of Nelson, set a short way back from the river, has Twin Bluffs (south edge of town, overlooking the Twin Bluffs Cafe) and a cheese factory where you can enjoy an assortment of Wisconsin cheeses and ice cream. Hang gliding from the bluff tops is a sport of increasing popularity here (but not for me).

A hard left at Nelson and State Highway 35 heads west through the Tiffany Bottoms Wildlife Area at the mouth of the Chippewa River. During the late 19th-century logging era, vast quantities of logs were floated down the Chippewa to the Mississippi. Many thousands of years earlier, glacial debris, carried down the Chippewa, formed a natural dam on the Mississippi, creating Lake Pepin. Ringed by high bluffs, the lake is 22 miles long and varies from one to nearly three miles in width.

William Cullen Bryant, the 19th-century poet and journalist, was an avid admirer of Lake Pepin, declaring that the region "ought to be visited in the summer by every poet and painter in the land." Good advice; it's one of the most beauti-ful spots in Wisconsin.

Six miles above the Chippewa is the village of Pepin. Laura Ingalls Wilder, author of the enormously popular *Little House* books, was born in a log cabin near here, on February 7, 1867. The first in her series of eight books, which she began writing at age 65, was *Little House in the Big Woods*, describing her experiences in the Pepin area.

The Little House Wayside, with a replica log cabin marking Wilder's birth site, is located seven miles northwest of Pepin on County CC (pick it up at the west edge of town). Surrounded by cornfields and pastures, the three-room cabin exhibits family photos, letters, and documents pertinent to Wilder's life and career. The wayside has picnic tables and a pump that provides well water. It's the perfect place to read a chapter or two of a *Little House* book. You can buy one at the Pepin Historical Museum, on State Highway 35 in town. The museum features Laura Ingalls Wilder memorabilia, including a quilt that belonged to Laura, local-history artifacts, and a kitchen and bedroom with 19th-century furnishings.

A block or two farther north is the Depot Museum, housed in an 1886 railroad depot that was moved from the riverfront to Laura Ingalls Wilder Park. You'll get a homespun guided tour of exhibits that include railroad memorabilia, river lore, models, relics, and other local-history items.

Downtown, along the waterfront, the Harbor View Cafe has an ever-changing menu of gourmet dishes that rivals many big-city restaurants. One of the cafe's two dining rooms features a small bookshop—bless their hearts!

It should come as no surprise that tiny Stockholm (population 89), the next village along the way, was settled by Swedes. Memorabilia from the early settlers is preserved at the Stockholm Institute, in the old post office. Next door is the Merchant's Hotel, established in 1864, where you can rent a room or the entire hotel (three rooms). There's an antique

shop in the hotel as well as a couple of others in town. Amish
Country specializes in museum-quality quilts and furniture
produced by Amish craftsmen. The village holds an art fair in
the park along the river on the third Saturday in July.

Continuing northwestward, the river, the railroad, and the
Great River Road all make a sharp swing to the west at the
hamlet of Maiden Rock. Lake Pepin is at its widest here, and
the scenery becomes even more beautiful, if that's possible.

But before the village comes the rock. According to leg-
end, a young and beautiful Sioux maiden, forbidden by her
family to marry the man she loved, leapt to her death from the
top of the bluff rather than marry another man she did not
love. There's a scenic overlook below the legendary bluff and
a historical marker with an account of the poignant tale.

Maiden Rock (village) stands at the mouth of the Rush
River, where it joins the Mississippi. I spent the closing hours
of a warm autumn afternoon here, sipping coffee and munch-
ing freshly baked cookies on the porch of the Harrisburg Inn
(bed-and-breakfast), while bald eagles frolicked above Lake
Pepin (we counted six in all) and a towboat pushed a long
string of barges upriver into the setting sun. A nice way to
end the day.

Downtown, Maiden Lane Shops, a small collection of
shops in an old creamery building, offer such staples as fudge,
antiques, and books.

Leaving Maiden Rock, the Great River Road climbs a
steep hill covered with maple, birch, and poplar trees. It then
continues to wind through a woodland landscape dotted with
small farms, offering occasional glimpses of the river off (and
down) to the left.

Four miles above Bay City, which marks the head of Lake
Pepin, is a wayside overlooking an obviously man-made boulder alignment on a distant bluff. Turn-of-the-century archae-
ologists interpreted the stones' pattern as a drawn bow and
arrow, aimed toward Lake Pepin. Today's archaeological

school of thought sees it as a bird effigy. Truth is, no one knows what it is, who built it, when, or why. So your guess is as good as any.

Northward. Hager City and Diamond Bluff (a sign and a few houses tucked between the railroad tracks and the river) slide by and the road turns away from the Mississippi, scampering up and down through a rolling landscape of hay fields, silos, and dairy barns, where pumpkins and squash are sold from roadside stands in autumn.

A dozen miles later, State Highway 35 moves down a long hill into Prescott, at the confluence of the St. Croix and the Mississippi Rivers.

A Prescott tourism publication urges visitors to "Look up and you may see a bald eagle flying overhead." I did and saw two, soaring above the junction of the rivers at high noon. I was suitably impressed.

From Mercord Park, downtown by the bridge, you can see a distinct change in color, where the Mississippi and St. Croix meet, and a series of standing wavelets as the Mississippi swallows the St. Croix. There's good fishing here, and a neat counterbalance railroad lift bridge, with massive iron work high overhead, spans the St. Croix. The Welcome and Heritage Center has visitor information and exhibits about Prescott's history.

If you're a football fan, River Falls, where the NFL's Kansas City Chiefs hold their summer training camp, is another 13 miles along State Highway 35.

But Prescott marks the northern terminus of Wisconsin's Great River Road. And we've reached the end of the line!

For More Information

La Crosse Area Convention and Visitors Bureau: 608-782-2366 or 800-658-9424

G. Heileman Brewery (La Crosse): 800-433-2337

Hixon House (La Crosse): 608-782-1980

Swarthout Museum (La Crosse): 608-782-1980

Great River State Trail: 800-873-1901

La Crosse River State Trail: 800-658-9424

Piggy's on Front Street (La Crosse): 608-784-4877

The Freight House (La Crosse): 608-784-6211

Trempealeau Chamber of Commerce: 608-534-6780

Trempealeau Hotel: 608-534-6898

Perrot State Park: 608-534-6409

Rock in the House (Fountain City): 608-687-6106 or 608-687-3553

Merrick State Park: 608-687-4936

Laue House Inn (Alma): 608-685-4923

Gallery House Bed and Breakfast (Alma): 608-685-4975

Sherman House (Alma): 608-685-4929

Pepin Visitor Information Center: 715-442-3011

Pepin Historical Museum: 715-442-3011

Depot Museum, Laura Ingalls Wilder Park (Pepin): 715-442-3011

Harbor View Cafe (Pepin): 715-442-3893

Merchant's Hotel (Stockholm): 715-442-2113 or 715-448-2508

Amish Country (Stockholm): 715-442-2015 or 800-247-7657

Harrisburg Inn (Maiden Rock): 715-448-4500

Welcome and Heritage Center (Prescott): 715-262-4800 or 800-474-3723

6

A Southeast Loop

Getting there: From Chicago (approximately 75 miles), take U.S. Route 12 northwest to Lake Geneva.

From Milwaukee (approximately 50 miles), take I-43 southwest to U.S. Route 12 and travel southeast to Lake Geneva. The trip makes a loop through Walworth and Waukesha Counties.

Highlights: Resort towns; Lake Geneva and Victorian mansions; Williams Bay and Yerkes Astronomical Observatory; Delavan with circus history; Elkhorn and Watson's Wild West Museum; Eagle, Old World Wisconsin, and southern Kettle Moraine State Forest; East Troy and its Electric Railroad Museum. The driving distance is approximately 75 miles. Allow one day (two, if you plan to spend much time at Old World Wisconsin).

This tour begins at Lake Geneva, the busy, bustling resort city at the east end of Lake Geneva.

Tourism and Lake Geneva discovered each other in 1870, when a few well-to-do Chicago folks headed for Wisconsin to escape the heat of a big-city summer, and the village of Geneva (now Lake Geneva) inadvertently had its first "season." Not long after, bankers, attorneys, and captains of industry with names such as Wrigley (chewing gum), Swift (meat packing), Borden (dairy products), Marshall Field (department stores), and Morton (salt) began to build palatial summer estates along the shores of Lake Geneva. They were huge Victorian affairs, with turrets and towers and gingerbread and verandas, all surrounded by expanses of manicured green that ran down to the sparkling blue lake. Weekend guests came up from Chicago by rail—one train was named the "Millionaire's Special"—to be met in the lakeshore villages by sleek steam yachts, with flags flying and captains in neat dress blues to deliver them to their final destination. A nice life, don't you think?

Lake Geneva is still a favorite with folks from Chicago and Milwaukee.

At the south edge of the city of 6,000 (winter population), there's Big Foot Beach State Park, established in 1949 on land purchased from the Maytag family (household-appliance fame). Named after a Potawatomi Indian chief, it's the only Wisconsin state park totally within a city. There are hiking trails, a wooded family campground, and a 900-foot-long sand beach on Lake Geneva. Like the city, it's packed on summer weekends.

Just beyond Big Foot Beach, stop at the Convention and Visitors Bureau office to pick up information on area dining, lodging, and attractions. Then park the car and hop aboard the red-and-green trolley that circles the town and stops at boutiques, shops, galleries, and restaurants.

There are two ways to see the old-money mansions that still dot the unspoiled (mostly) lakeshore. One, you can walk. A public pathway that follows an old Potawatomi Indian trail encircles the entire lake (26 miles). Two, you can take a boat cruise.

Geneva Lake Cruise Line offers a wide variety of dinner, luncheon, and narrated sight-seeing cruises aboard replicas of early lake steamers. One of the most popular cruises is the Mail Boat Cruise. In summer, the line operates one of the few marine mail-delivery services in the country, delivering mail to lakeshore residents. The mail people (young, agile, fearless) jump off the boat onto each lakeshore home's dock, deliver the mail to a rural mailbox, then leap back aboard. No problem. Except the boat never stops! Timing is crucial, and most mail people have horror stories about wet piers, dogs, freshly painted docks, or jumping and literally missing the boat! Reservations are required for all cruises. Departures are from Lake Geneva's Riviera Docks, a former lakeshore ballroom done up in tan brick and red tile that's been converted to offices and a shopping arcade. It's worth a visit, even if you're not taking a cruise.

A stone's throw northwest of the Riviera Docks is Lake Geneva Beach, a public swimming area.

If you're thinking of staying awhile, the Geneva Inn, Grand Geneva Resort & Spa, and French Country Inn (bed-and-breakfast) are among many resorts and lodging establishments scattered around the perimeter of Lake Geneva that will meet your every rest-and-recreation requirement.

The Evergreen Theatre, a professional equity theater located at Grand Geneva Resort & Spa, offers dramas and comedies year-round, and you don't have to be a resort guest to attend a performance.

Head west from Lake Geneva on State Highway 50, which becomes a four-lane road as it climbs out of town and past the Geneva National Golf Club. Arnold Palmer and Lee Trevino designed the two 18-hole courses at this posh facility.

At the intersection with State Highway 67 (six miles), you may wish to make a one-mile detour south to the resort village of Williams Bay, famous as the home of the University of Chicago's Yerkes Astronomical Observatory. The observatory's 40-inch refractor telescope is the world's largest. The observatory is a real beauty, with enough stone arches, domes, columns, walkways, and balconies to do most state capitols proud. Some of the keenest scientific minds of this century have come here to use this telescope, including Albert Einstein, Edwin Hubble (namesake of the Hubble Space Telescope), and Carl Sagan. Tours are available on Saturdays.

Back on State Highway 50 and heading west, the road hurries through a landscape of small farms, country homes, and horse farms on the short drive to Delavan. Lake Lawn Resort (amenities include golf and an airstrip), on the shores of Lake Delavan at the east edge of town, occupies land that was once winter quarters for the Mabie Brothers U.S. Olympic Circus (1847), then the country's largest.

Between 1847 and 1894, there were 26 different circuses that called Delavan home, including the P. T. Barnum Menagerie (1871–1873).

Tower Park, on Walworth Avenue at the east end of the downtown district, was a center of Delavan's circus activity. Wagon and blacksmith shops lined the streets around the park, and many circus performers stayed at the Park Hotel, built in 1848, and still standing. The park has two historic markers—one at the base of a life-size fiberglass giraffe, the other on the base of an elephant—detailing the city's circus history.

The pachyderm is a likeness of Romeo, a 10,500-pound rogue elephant that traveled with the 1847 Mabie Brothers show. There's also a statue of a clown. If the face looks vaguely familiar, it was used on the five-cent American circus commemorative postage stamp, issued in 1966.

More than 100 members of the 19th-century circus colony are buried in Spring Grove and St. Andrews Cemeteries (south end of Seventh Street), including some of the biggest names in early circus history. Their graves are marked with metal placards.

Don't leave town without driving by the Allyn Mansion Inn, a 23-room Queen Anne/Eastlake mansion that defines the term Victorian. Listed on the National Register of Historic Places, the home was built in 1885 by Milwaukee architect

E. Townsend Mix and is now a bed-and-breakfast. If you wish to stay, its amenities include original walnut woodwork, frescoed ceilings, 10 marble fireplaces, three formal parlors, and two grand pianos.

From Delavan, follow State Highway 11 northeast on a pleasant country jaunt through a landscape dotted with wooded glacial ridges, fields of oats and corn, and farms sporting red barns and huge woodpiles.

Six miles along the way is Elkhorn, a small industrial city of 5,300, long known for the manufacture of band instruments. Joseph Philbrick Webster, a popular Civil War–era composer, wrote "The Sweet Bye and Bye" while living here. The Webster House Museum, the composer's home until his death in 1875, contains Webster memorabilia, the room where he wrote more than 1,000 hymns and ballads, and a 400-piece mounted bird collection. Watson's Wild West Museum, on the north edge of town, is filled with rootin' tootin' 1880s Western memorabilia.

Follow State Highway 67 north from Elkhorn through the hamlet of Little Prairie into the stony fields, rolling hills, and wooded glacial ridges of the southern Kettle Moraine State Forest. State forest headquarters are located three miles west of Eagle on State Highway 59. The visitors center offers films, museum exhibits, and information about the Ice Age glaciers and how they created this land called the Kettle Moraine.

Eagle is home to Old World Wisconsin, the State Historical Society's outdoor museum of living history. More than 50 original pioneer buildings have been moved here from across the state and have been grouped into ethnic farmsteads as well as a 19th-century crossroads village. Costumed interpreters demonstrate pioneer folkways. The museum is huge, covering nearly 600 acres. You can easily spend a day exploring. A tractor-pulled tram runs between the farmsteads, but even so, a fair amount of walking is required. Comfortable shoes are a must.

Continuing northward from Eagle, State Highway 67 winds around and climbs up and down wooded glacial hills, scurrying past barns with cobblestone foundations. The forest's Ottawa Lake Recreation Area, just west of State Highway 67 on County ZZ, offers fishing, swimming, boating, and camping. A half mile east on County ZZ, the Scuppermong Hiking and Ski Trail Area has 11 miles of hiking trails that wind through pine plantations, southern hardwoods, and ancient glacial features. To use either area, you'll need a park vehicle sticker, available at forest headquarters or the visitor contact stations at forest recreation areas.

Follow State Highway 67 north to the intersection with County D, and turn east (right) onto County D. You're out of the state forest now, but still in the Kettle Moraine. Upscale homes hide in the woods here, and more are in the works. The road slides gently up and down, and the leaves on the oaks along the way show their silver backs in any sort of breeze—a sign, according to weather folklore, that rain is on the way. The mood here is easygoing, genteel.

Genesee Depot (six miles) has more shady streets and Victorian houses. The village is famous as the site of Ten Chimneys (a few miles outside of town), the longtime estate of the late husband-and-wife acting team Alfred Lunt and Lynn Fontanne, who performed together in more than 140 Broadway plays. Lunt, a Genesee Depot native, and Fontanne used the estate as a retreat, a summer home, and a studio for rehearsals with fellow actors such as Laurence Olivier, Vivien Leigh, Helen Hayes, Clifton Webb, and Alexander Woollcott.

From Genesee Depot, follow State Highway 83 south through the lush, rolling farmland to Mukwonago. Signs offering pumpkins, onions, potatoes, and squash for sale (in season) pop up here and there along the way, and tall oaks line the fencerows between the farm fields.

Continue driving on State Highway 83 to the south edge of Mukwonago, and turn right onto County ES. Just beyond

Phantom Lake is The Elegant Farmer, Wisconsin's largest farm market. Apples, berries, and all sorts of fruit, in season; it's pick your own, if you like. There's a farm deli offering fresh-baked breads, fresh fruit muffins, and other mouth-watering taste treats.

Continue southward on County ES. Running beside this country road is one of the last electrified rail lines in Wisconsin. Inter-urban trolleys once connected many of southeastern Wisconsin's outlying communities to Milwaukee. They're gone now, but the memories (and some working trolleys) remain at the East Troy Electric Railroad Museum.

Follow County ES into East Troy, and watch for Church Street and signs pointing to the museum, which features exhibits and artifacts from the inter-urban days. Ten-mile-long trolley rides are available on weekend afternoons from spring through autumn.

There's another throwback to the good old days at J. Lauber's, a 1920s ice-cream parlor adjacent to the museum. A four-page menu of ice-cream treats includes 20 flavors of malts. There's a huge, old-fashioned candy counter and a jukebox that plays 78-rpm. records.

Before you leave East Troy, check the playbill at the Alpine Valley Music Theatre, located south of town on County D. Some of the biggest headliners in popular music are featured during the summer season (outdoors).

When it's time to head home, you can pick up I-43 and scamper back to Milwaukee or Beloit or take State Highway 120 south to Lake Geneva, where U.S. Route 12 leads back to Chicago.

For More Information

Big Foot Beach State Park: 414-248-2528

Lake Geneva Convention and Visitors Bureau: 414-248-4416 or 800-345-1020

Geneva Lake Cruise Line (Lake Geneva): 414-248-6206 or 800-558-5911

Geneva Inn (Lake Geneva): 414-248-5680 or 800-441-5881

Grand Geneva Resort & Spa (Lake Geneva): 414-248-8811 or 800-558-3417

French Country Inn (Lake Geneva): 414-245-5220

Yerkes Astronomical Observatory (Williams Bay): 414-245-5555

Delavan–Delavan Lake Chamber of Commerce: 414-728-5095 or 800-624-0052

Lake Lawn Resort (Delavan): 414-728-5511 or 800-338-5253

Allyn Mansion Inn (Delavan): 414-728-9090

Webster House Museum (Elkhorn): 414-723-4248

Watson's Wild West Museum (Elkhorn): 414-723-7505

Kettle Moraine State Forest–Southern Unit: 414-594-6200

Old World Wisconsin (Eagle): 414-594-6300

The Elegant Farmer (Mukwonago): 414-363-6770

East Troy Electric Railroad Museum: 414-548-3837

J. Lauber's (East Troy): 414-642-3679

Alpine Valley Music Theatre (East Troy): 414-642-4400

7

Northern Kettle Moraine

Getting there: From Chicago (approximately 120 miles), take I-94 north to Milwaukee, then continue west for 25 miles to State Highway 83.

From Milwaukee (approximately 25 miles), take I-94 west to State Highway 83.

Highlights: Beautiful glacial scenery and northern Kettle Moraine State Forest; North Lake and Kettle Moraine Railway; Hartford, Pike Lake State Park, and Hartford Heritage Auto Museum; West Bend with West Bend Art Museum; Dundee and Henry S. Reuss Ice Age Visitor Center; Greenbush and Wade House and Wesley Jung Carriage Museum. The driving distance is approximately 70 miles. Allow one day, minimum.

Climbing, weaving, and winding over, around, and through Wisconsin's beautiful glacial landscape, the Kettle Moraine Scenic Drive is not for someone in a hurry. Indeed, much of the route is posted well below the normal speed limit.

In the mists of the ancient past, much of present-day Wisconsin was covered by a vast sheet of ice that was, in places, more than a mile thick. As the glacier crept southward, four huge lobes moved outward from the main ice sheet like frigid fingers extending from an icy palm. About 22,000 years ago, two of these lobes bumped into each other in what is today southeastern Wisconsin. When the pushing, shoving, grinding, and grating was finished and the ice melted (12,000 years ago, give or take a few millennia), the future Badger State was left with a magnificent collection of rolling hills, steep ridges, sparkling lakes, and gumdrop-shaped mounds. Known as the Kettle Moraine—"kettle" for the cuplike depressions common throughout the region and "moraine" for the gravel ridges left behind at the edge of the ice sheet— this unique glacial landscape extends north-south for more than 100 miles.

We'll travel a dozen or more country roads on this journey through the northern Kettle Moraine. The way is marked by white-and-green acorn-shaped signs pointing out "Kettle Moraine Scenic Drive."

We begin in Waukesha County, at the intersection of State Highway 83 and I-94, about 25 miles west of downtown Milwaukee, and head north. After the Civil War, well-to-do Milwaukeeans began to move out into the country, and summer colonies grew up around many of the Kettle Moraine's shimmering lakes. In the village of Chenequa, on the shores of Pine Lake, you'll see some beautiful old homes (and some dandy new ones, too) in the woods along the lakeshore.

Kettle Moraine Scenic Drive slides in from the west via County K at the north end of Pike Lake, joining State Highway 83 for the brief journey to North Lake, a pleasant Victorian village standing beside the lake bearing the same name. If you're here on a summer Sunday or autumn weekend, the Kettle Moraine Railway will take you on a nostalgic eight-mile round-trip through the forests of the Kettle Moraine.

Turn right on County VV at the north end of the village, head east a mile to County E and turn left (mind the Kettle Moraine Scenic Drive signs), heading northward past cornfields and pastures nestled between tree-lined ridges left behind by the glacier.

Tiny Monches marks the end of Waukesha County and the beginning of Washington County, where County K becomes the Kettle Moraine Scenic Drive (a mere formality, as only the road signs change).

Continuing northward through Erin Township (Emerald Road, Dublin Drive, Shamrock Lane, a cluster of houses called Erin Meadows), the road runs past farms and fields dotted with small kettle lakes and ponds. Is it my imagination or are the farm fields here a deep emerald green?

The twin steeples, growing larger on the horizon, belong to Holy Hill, one of the most picturesque religious shrines in the Midwest. In the late 1850s, a huge wooden cross was erected atop the hill. Tradition says a recluse who lived on the hill and worshipped at the cross experienced a miraculous cure. Devout pilgrims were drawn to the spot, a custom that continues to this day. Officially, Holy Hill is the National Shrine of Mary and is staffed by the Discalced Carmelite Order of Friars. Both church and grounds welcome visitors year-round (the original wooden cross may be viewed in the vestibule of the lower church).

North of Holy Hill, the scenic drive turns right onto Waterford Road and climbs a steep hill to the top of a ridge. Stone fences are along the way here, some old and collapsed, others in good repair. Stones are also a legacy of the glaciers, unhappily for farmers who had to clear each field by hand to prepare it for the plow. But the glacial debris did provide a ready source of building material. Most barns, and many houses, have cobblestone foundations; occasionally, you'll see a stone silo or small stone outbuildings.

At the top of the hill, the scenic drive turns north (left) onto Kettle Moraine Road, winding past two segments of the Ice Age Trail, the Holy Hill section, and, just up the road at Pike Lake State Park, the Pike Lake segment. The national scenic trail follows the glacier's terminal moraine (the farthest advance of the ice), rambling across the state for nearly 1,000 miles.

Popular Pike Lake State Park offers fishing, family camping, swimming, picnic facilities, and hiking trails. Powder Hill, a kame (hill) left by the glacier (formed when water from the melting glacier poured through a funnel-like opening in the ice and mounded up gravel, much like sand in an hourglass), is 1,350 feet above sea level, one of the highest points around.

North of Pike Lake, the scenic drive joins State Highway 60 and turns east. A short detour to the west leads to Hartford where, from 1906 to 1931, a luxury automobile called the Kissel was manufactured. Celebrities such as singer Al Jolson and aviator Amelia Earhart drove Kissels; Earhart nicknamed hers the "Yellow Peril." The Hartford Heritage Auto Museum has a large collection of Kissels, as well as Nash autos (also manufactured in Wisconsin), and other rare motor cars. W. B. Place, a Hartford tannery dating from 1866, offers beautiful leather items in its retail store.

From Pike Lake, follow State Highway 60 east four miles to Slinger, a community of 2,340, which began life in 1845 as Schleisingerville (say it three times quickly!). The name was changed in 1921. Watch for the Kettle Moraine Scenic Drive signs at the west edge of town, and turn north on State Highway 144. Cream-colored brick homes and commercial buildings are plentiful downtown. The village is served by an active railroad, but the old depot now houses a construction firm's offices.

Continuing northward, the scenic drive follows State Highway 144 along the west side of Big Cedar Lake. Both the lakeshore and the winding road are lined with homes and summer cottages. No scenic-drive signs mark the way for the next few miles, but you're on the right track.

A few miles north of Big Cedar Lake, State Highway 144 joins State Highway 33 and swings east into the city of West

Bend. Go straight ahead, across State Highway 33 onto Glacier Drive, following the Kettle Moraine Scenic Drive along the west and northwest fringes of West Bend on a laundry list of roads. Except for the State Highway 33/144 intersection, the route is well marked. But just in case: follow Glacier Drive north one mile, and turn right onto Schuster Road; follow Schuster east one mile to Kettleview Drive, and turn left; go north one mile (cross Beaver Dam Road) to County D, and turn right; take County D east past Good Luck Road (a dead end) to Lighthouse Lane, and turn left. After some 200 yards, you'll come to the intersection of Sleepy Hollow Road (a four-way stop). Go straight ahead for a quarter mile, past the bowling alley and over the little bridge to Kettle Moraine Scenic Drive, and turn left. Easy as pie. (Well, I did go astray at the State Highway 33/144 intersection.)

If you're a shopper/bargain hunter, you'll want to stop in West Bend. There are many factory outlets here, with leather goods, kitchenware, sportswear, and small household appliances heading a long list of bargains. The West Bend Art Museum is noted for its collection of early Wisconsin art and works by German–American artist Carl von Marr, whose painting, *The Flagellants*, depicting the height of the Dark Ages, is the largest oil painting in Wisconsin at 15.5 by 23.5 feet!

Back on the scenic drive. Our country road heads northward along a flat prairie bordered by glacial hills and ridges on the east, passing farms with cream-colored brick homes, red barns with cobblestone foundations, and concrete silos. Ducks, and occasionally Canada geese, often feed and rest in the small kettle ponds and cattail swamps along the way. With a loop past Smith Lake, the scenic drive crosses County H and enters the Northern Unit of the Kettle Moraine State Forest.

Spread across parts of three counties, the 28,000-acre forest was established to protect and preserve some of the Kettle Moraine's most spectacular glacial features. Private lands, including farms, homes, and municipalities, lie within forest boundaries, so you can drive through and conduct normal business without an admission fee. But if you stop to use state forest recreation areas, picnic facilities, or hiking trails, you'll need a park vehicle sticker. One-day stickers (inexpensive) are available at recreation areas.

The ridges and rolling hills become more distinctive here, and the hardwood forest grows thicker. Winding and twisting, the scenic drive zigs left and zags right onto County S, scooting through the hamlet of New Fane. A picturesque church built of cobblestones stands a mile north of town, beside a 19th-century church cemetery.

Kettle Moraine geological features

Just beyond the church, the scenic drive turns left onto County GGG, and a five-minute drive brings you to Mauthe Lake Recreation Area, where there's camping, fishing, hiking, swimming, and a lovely picnic area beside the lake.

North of Mauthe Lake, County GGG joins County SS and the scenic drive swings west into New Prospect, a village serving the campers, hikers, and fisherfolk who use the forest. A half mile beyond the village, turn right on County G, and head north along a flat outwash plain bordered on the west by crevasse fills (ridges formed when glacial debris filled in huge fissures in the ice).

Some of the Kettle Moraine's glacial landscape was carved by the ice itself, some of it was sculpted by torrents of water pouring off the dying glacier—fascinating stuff, but a little complex. Stop at the Henry S. Reuss Ice Age Visitor Center, at the intersection of County G and State Highway 67, where exhibits and a film explain how the Kettle Moraine came into being. There's a marvelous view of the glacial landscape from the visitors center veranda and the nearby Moraine Ridge Nature Trail.

From the center, take State Highway 67 east a half mile to the village of Dundee, and follow the Kettle Moraine Scenic Drive east on County F. The tall, gumdrop-shaped hill to the left is Dundee Mountain, a kame standing 255 feet high. There's a smaller kame off to the right that's said to be one of the most photographed features in the forest.

At Dundee Mountain, turn left on Division Road, and travel north one mile to Butler Lake Road and the entrance to the Long Lake Recreation Area. More camping, fishing, swimming, picnicking, and hiking here and, if you're really ambitious, a trail leading to the top of Dundee Mountain.

Follow Butler Lake Road east one mile, and turn into the parking lot at the "Butler Lake" sign. Here, you'll find an esker, which is a sharp, narrow gravel ridge formed by a stream flowing through a tunnel beneath the ice. When the glacier melted away, the gravel carried by the stream slumped to leave this ridge. Steps lead to a hiking trail along the top of the formation, which is four miles long.

A short distance past Butler Lake, the scenic drive turns right onto County V, then north onto Shamrock Road, winding and twisting past two large, tree-covered kames before swinging right onto Woodside Road and, soon after, County U. More boulders along the roadside here, cleared from the fields and piled in the fencerows. After a winding mile, turn left (north) onto County A, where there's a picnic area and a trail leading to a tall observation tower standing high on a glacial ridge.

Three miles north of the tower, the scenic drive turns left onto State Highway 67 for a half mile, then right on Kettle Moraine Scenic Drive past flat farm fields and planted pine plantations to the Greenbush Recreation Area. There are picnic facilities and hiking trails here, plus the Greenbush Kettle, the Kettle Moraine's largest and most outstanding example of these cuplike depressions, which were formed when huge blocks of ice buried in the glacial debris melted away. The glacial ice was so compact that it melted about one inch every 100 years. That gives you some idea of how long it took to form the Greenbush Kettle, which is a couple of hundred feet deep.

Up and down, around and over for a couple of miles, and the scenic drive slides onto County T. Neat stone fences and glistening white buildings welcome you to the village of Greenbush and the State Historical Society's Wade House and Wesley Jung Carriage Museum. A stagecoach inn constructed between 1847 and 1851, Wade House stands halfway between Sheboygan and Fond du Lac and was an important stop along the plank road that ran between the two cities. Guided tours led by costumed guides include demonstrations of 19th-century folkways. The site's carriage museum houses Wisconsin's largest collection of restored horse- and hand-drawn carriages.

From Greenbush, it's 12 miles east to Sheboygan and I-43 or 12 miles west to Fond du Lac and U.S. Route 41, either of which leads to Milwaukee or Green Bay.

For More Information

Kettle Moraine Railway (North Lake): 414-782-8074

Holy Hill National Shrine of Mary (Hubertus): 414-628-1838

Pike Lake State Park: 414-670-3400

Hartford Area Chamber of Commerce: 414-673-7002

Hartford Heritage Auto Museum: 414-673-7999

W. B. Place (Hartford): 414-673-3130 or 800-826-4433

West Bend Art Museum: 414-334-9638

Kettle Moraine State Forest–Northern Unit: 414-626-2116

Henry S. Reuss Ice Age Visitor Center (Campbellsport): 920-533-8322

Wade House and Wesley Jung Carriage Museum (Greenbush): 414-526-3271

8

A Lakeshore Drive

Getting there: From Chicago (approximately 145 miles), take I-94 north to Milwaukee and I-43 north to Sheboygan; State Highway 23 leads into downtown Sheboygan.

From Milwaukee (approximately 52 miles), take I-43 north to Sheboygan.

Highlights: Lakeshore scenery; Sheboygan and the John Michael Kohler Arts Center; Kohler, the Kohler Design Center, and the American Club Resort; Manitowoc with the Wisconsin Maritime Museum; Two Rivers, Rogers Street Fishing Village, and Point Beach State Forest; Kewaunee and the Kewaunee County Historical Museum; Algoma and the von Stiehl Winery. The total driving distance is approximately 60 miles. Allow a day, minimum.

This tour begins in Sheboygan, a lakeshore city famous for its bratwurst, the delicious spicy sausage brought to Wisconsin by German immigrants. Locals eat brats on a hard roll, topped with German mustard and plenty of pickles and onions. Add to that a side order of potato salad and a cold brew, and you're in for some good eating (just don't count the calories).

Downtown, along Riverfront Drive, a boardwalk over-looks a collection of historic commercial fishing shanties along the Sheboygan River—many house restaurants, art galleries, and retail shops. In nearby Deland Park, on the lakeshore a stone's throw north of the river, you can see the remains of the *Lottie Cooper*, a three-masted schooner that sank just offshore in 1894 during a fierce Lake Michigan storm.

Sheboygan is home to the highly regarded John Michael Kohler Arts Center, featuring contemporary American sculpture, crafts, photography, and the work of grassroots artists. The complex includes an elegant 1892 Italianate villa that was the original home of J. M. Kohler, an Austrian immigrant who founded the plumbing-ware firm that still bears his name.

In 1917, Kohler's son, Walter, and the Olmsted Brothers (they planned New York's Central Park and the Harvard University campus) built the model village of Kohler around a plumbing-ware factory four miles west of Sheboygan (follow State Highway 23 west). Here, you can tour Waelderhaus, a replica of Kohler's ancestral home in Bregenzerwald, Austria, and visit the Kohler Design Center, which showcases company products in more colors and styles than you could ever imagine. There's also a museum of company history and ceramic arts. Exhibits include a Kohler powered generator (the firm also manufactures small engines) used at Little America station in Antarctica by Admiral Richard Byrd, along with a flag that Byrd carried to both the North and South Poles. Make arrangements here for a tour of the plumbing-ware factory. Close by is the American Club Resort, once a dormitory for immigrant workers and today a plush, five-diamond resort hotel (great bathrooms). Other attractions include Kohler Woodlake, a collection of stylish shops, and the Blackwolf Run Golf Course, designed by Pete Dye.

Back in Sheboygan, follow Fifteenth Street north from Kohler Memorial Drive (State Highway 23). The street becomes Lakeshore Road at the north end of town, and eventually, County LS.

Heading north along a flat lakeshore bluff top, with shimmering Lake Michigan a mile or so off to the right, County LS slides past dairy farms (some with "Potatoes for Sale" signs) and long, narrow plantations of pine trees, planted to help hold the sandy soil in place.

Ten miles along the way, the road slides through the village of Cleveland. Hika Park is a spot to dip your toe in Lake Michigan or pause for a picnic.

Another 10 miles brings us to Manitowoc (population 32,500), a city with a long and rich maritime heritage. County LS becomes South Tenth Street at the edge of the city and leads straight to the downtown harbor area.

Manitowoc is the Wisconsin port for the SS *Badger*, which shuttles passengers and autos across the lake to Ludington, Michigan, from mid-May to early October. Built as a railroad car ferry in 1952, the 410-foot *Badger* is the last remaining passenger steamship on the Great Lakes. The ship has a capacity of 620 passengers and 130 autos, with staterooms, two restaurants, a retail shop, a maritime museum, and a movie theater to help pass the time during the 60-mile, four-hour crossing. It's the closest thing to an ocean voyage that you'll find in these parts.

Manitowoc's shipbuilding tradition began in 1847 with the construction of the schooner *Citizen*. Shipyards proliferated and, between 1847 and 1899, when the *Cora A.*, the last schooner built on the Great Lakes, was launched, more than 100 wooden sailing ships had been built here.

As sail gave way to the age of steam and steel, smaller shipyards fell by the way, and the Manitowoc Shipbuilding Company became preeminent. During World War II, at the request of President Franklin Roosevelt, the firm built 28 fleet submarines for the U.S. Navy, employing 7,000 workers in three shifts, seven days a week, at the peak of production.

It was a time when farmers worked their fields by day and built ships by night, and eager young navy crews came to the Midwest to take delivery of their freshwater-built submarines.

After launching and sea trials, the subs were placed aboard special floating dry docks and towed to New Orleans via the Illinois–Mississippi Waterway, heading to war in the Pacific. The Manitowoc-built USS *Rasher* sank 99,901 tons of enemy shipping during the war, the second highest total for an American submarine.

Following the war, Manitowoc Shipbuilding resumed the production of Great Lakes freighters, producing a total of 437 hulls of all types during its long history in Manitowoc.

Exhibits at the Wisconsin Maritime Museum, on the lakeshore at the mouth of the Manitowoc River, tell the story of the city's rich maritime history through artifacts, exquisite ship models, videos, and a World War II submarine. Tools and items from the wooden-ship era include a full-size cross section of a wooden schooner hull, constructed with old-time techniques. A re-creation of the 19th-century port of Manitowoc features full-size facades of businesses involved in the shipping industry.

Of many exhibits devoted to the Manitowoc-built submarines, the largest is the USS *Cobia*, a World War II sub (ironically, not built here). Guided tours provide glimpses into the claustrophobic world of the submariner, where 80 men lived in unbelievably close intimacy for weeks on end (with one shower per week).

After your museum visit, head for Beerntsen's Confectionery, a block west of the museum on Eighth Street, for ice-cream treats and delectable, hand-dipped chocolates. These are served in an old-fashioned ice-cream parlor and candy store founded in 1932.

Other Manitowoc attractions you may wish to visit include the Rahr-West Museum, with collections of 19- and 20th-century art, porcelain, ivory carvings, Native American relics, and dolls. Zunker's Antique Car Museum has some 40 autos, along with an antique gas station and other memorabilia that will excite auto buffs.

Follow winding Maritime Drive north from the Wisconsin Maritime Museum past the marina (neat stuff in the ship's store) to the junction with State Highway 42. For the six miles between Manitowoc and Two Rivers (you really can't tell where one city ends and the other begins), the road runs close to Lake Michigan. A wayside and several scenic overlooks provide spots to pull over and watch the lake and its ever-changing moods.

With a sweeping left turn and a swoop over the West Twin River, State Highway 42 eases into downtown Two Rivers. A few commercial fishermen still work from this port, and the city of 13,000 is a major sportfishing center (lake trout, chinook salmon), as witnessed by all those charter fishing boats moored in the West Twin River. Two Rivers is also famous as the home of the ice-cream sundae, which was created here in 1881 and originally sold only on Sunday. Berners Ice Cream Parlor, in the restored Washington House, an 1850s workingman's hotel preserved as a museum, will sell you a sundae or soda any day of the week (Jefferson Street).

As State Highway 42 crosses the East Twin River at Twenty-second Street, you can see the commercial-fishing docks. Also along the river here is the Rogers Street Fishing Village, which is listed on the National Register of Historic Places. Museum exhibits include artifacts of commercial fishing and shipwrecks.

Back on Twenty-second Street, continue east to County O, a block or so beyond where State Highway 42 turns north. On the right is Neshotah Park, with picnic areas, playground equipment, and a fine stretch of Lake Michigan beach.

Four miles north on County O is Point Beach State Forest, with five miles of Lake Michigan beach, hiking trails, wooded campsites, and beachfront picnic areas.

Rawley Point Lighthouse, standing tall on the beach near the forest's visitor contact station, was established in 1853 and still warns ships away from the treacherous waters off the point. The present light tower was built in 1894—its light can be seen up to 19 miles away. The small, brick light keeper's quarters at the base of the tower were part of the original lighthouse (no tours). Before the lighthouse was built, the waters around Rawley Point were a graveyard of ships, with more than two dozen vessels wrecked or sunk here, including the famed "Christmas Tree Ship."

In November 1912, the schooner *Rouse Simmons*, heading down the lake for Chicago with a huge load of Christmas trees, disappeared with all hands during a fierce autumn gale. The following spring, commercial fishermen from Two Rivers brought up hundreds of trees in their nets, and it was assumed the vessel had gone down somewhere off that port. In 1924, 12 years after the *Simmons* disappeared, a wallet belonging to her skipper was raised in a fisherman's net, and the Christmas Tree Ship became part of Great Lakes folklore. Scuba divers found her remains in 1970, about eight miles off Rawley Point, sitting more or less upright on the bottom in 180 feet of water. There were still Christmas trees in her hold!

Pieces of old shipwrecks occasionally wash ashore to this day. The broken and battered bow section of an old schooner is displayed at the forest's visitor contact station.

From Point Beach, follow County O north, then west as it becomes County V, intersecting with State Highway 42 about five minutes after leaving Point Beach.

Heading north on State Highway 42, you'll come to the Point Beach Nuclear Power Plant. Exhibits at the Point Beach Energy Center include audiovisual displays about alternative energy sources, computer games, and a model nuclear reactor large enough to walk into. There's a half-mile-long nature trail on the grounds.

Hurrying along through flat, bluff-top farmlands, with Lake Michigan a mile off to the right, State Highway 42 scampers through the village of Two Creeks before you can say the name. There's a rare eight-sided barn on the left side of the road a short distance north of the village. Located a bit farther, just past the Kewaunee County line, the concrete-gray and turquoise Art Deco–style lakeshore buildings are the Kewaunee Nuclear Power Plant (closed to visitors).

A few miles farther north, State Highway 42 makes an "S" curve, turning first toward the lake, then swinging left and sweeping downhill into Kewaunee (population 2,750).

Lots of history here. Jacques Marquette, the renowned Jesuit missionary and explorer, paid a visit in 1673. A century later, fur traders built posts at the mouth of the Kewaunee River. Railroad-car ferry service across Lake Michigan began here in 1892, when the Ann Arbor Railroad's *Carferry No. 1* loaded 22 cars full of flour to be transported across Lake Michigan. The service was later extended to other ports and continued until 1990, when the last railroad-car ferry sailed from Kewaunee.

On Courthouse Square, the Kewaunee County Historical Museum has local-history exhibits in a building that formerly housed the sheriff's office, residence, and county jail (open Memorial Day through Labor Day). You may also want to visit the Besadny Anadromous Fish Facility, three miles west of town, to see fish migrations (in season) and spawn collection. Before leaving town, check out the harbor and the Kewaunee Pierhead Light. With its peaked roofs and dormers, it looks like something from Hansel and Gretel.

State Highway 42 crosses the Kewaunee River at the harbor on its way north out of town, climbing a long hill and riding the bluff tops north to Alaska. No snowcapped mountains here, but the tiny, unincorporated village boasts an East Alaska Lake and a West Alaska Lake and a golf course that borders both sides of the highway (watch out for stray golf

balls!). Just beyond Alaska, the road settles in beside Lake
Michigan for the six-mile journey to Algoma.

Algoma is a pretty lakeshore town and a sportfishing hot
spot, with several charter-boat operators who will be happy to
take you in search of the big ones.

Local folks and businesses donated the material and the
labor to build the slick new visitors information center on
Lake Street (State Highway 42) at the south edge of town.
Pick up brochures, maps, and information on Algoma and
northeast Wisconsin here, and ask about the guided walking
tours of the historic downtown area.

Follow Lake Street as it angles to the right and the waterfront. Algoma's north pierhead light was established in 1893.
The present light tower, painted a brilliant red, dates from
1932 and contains a fog signal that sounds every 10 seconds
when visibility falls under two miles. Fishing shanties and
charter boats line the banks of the Ahanpee River, which emp-
ties into the harbor, and a scenic walkway along the river provides great views of all the activity. Close by, the von Stiehl
Winery offers tastings of its fruit wines and tours of the winery. Among the winery's gift-shop offerings are 16 flavors of
fudge, homemade, of course, "with real cream and butter."
Oh, go ahead!

Our Lake Michigan lakeshore drive ends here, but Door
County is just up the road, so follow State Highway 42,
County S, or County U (the scenic drive along the lake).

For More Information

Sheboygan County Convention and Visitors Bureau:
   920-457-9495 or 800-457-9497

John Michael Kohler Arts Center (Sheboygan): 920-458-6144

Waelderhaus (Kohler): 920-452-4079

Kohler Design Center: 920-457-3699

American Club Resort (Kohler): 920-457-8000 or 800-344-2838

Manitowoc Visitor and Convention Bureau: 920-683-4388 or 800-627-4896

SS *Badger*, Lake Michigan Carferry: 800-841-4243

Wisconsin Maritime Museum (Manitowoc): 920-684-0218

Beerntsen's Confectionery (Manitowoc): 920-684-9616

Rahr-West Museum (Manitowoc): 920-683-4501

Zunker's Antique Car Museum (Manitowoc): 920-684-4005

Berners Ice Cream Parlor/Historic Washington House (Two Rivers): 920-793-2490

Rogers Street Fishing Village (Two Rivers): 920-793-5905

Point Beach State Forest: 920-794-9480

Point Beach Energy Center (Two Rivers): 920-755-6400

Kewaunee Chamber of Commerce: 920-388-4822 or 800-666-8214

Kewaunee County Historical Museum: 920-388-4410

Besadny Anadromous Fish Facility (Kewaunee): 920-388-1025

Algoma Area Chamber of Commerce: 920-487-2041 or 800-498-4888

Von Stiehl Winery (Algoma): 920-487-5208 or 800-955-5208

9

A Door County Sampler

Getting there: From Chicago (approximately 235 miles), take I-94 north to Milwaukee, then I-43 north to Green Bay, and State Highway 57 northeast to Sturgeon Bay. Or pick up State Highway 42 near Two Rivers, and follow it north to Sturgeon Bay.

From Milwaukee (approximately 140 miles), take I-43 north to Green Bay, and follow State Highway 57 northeast to Sturgeon Bay. Or pick up State Highway 42 near Two Rivers, and follow it north to Sturgeon Bay.

From Minneapolis–St. Paul (approximately 325 miles), take I-94 east to State Highway 29 (just beyond Menomonie, Wis.), and follow State Highway 29 east to Green Bay. Take U.S. Route 41 north, and follow the Sturgeon Bay signs around and through Green Bay to State Highway 57. The trip makes a loop through the Door County peninsula.

Highlights: Lake Michigan and Green Bay, with sandy beaches, picturesque Victorian coastal hamlets, apple and cherry orchards, state parks, lighthouses, and Washington Island. The driving distance is approximately 275 miles. Allow two days, minimum.

Straddling a 70-mile-long peninsula that juts off the mainland like the thumb on a mitten, Door County is Wisconsin's Great Lakes playground, bordered on the west by the bay of Green Bay and on the east by Lake Michigan.

The first tourists arrived by steamer in the 1890s, visiting coastal hamlets whose very names speak the essence of Victorian gentility—Sturgeon Bay, Egg Harbor, Ephraim, Sister Bay, Death's Door.

Death's Door? Early French explorers named the passage between Green Bay and Lake Michigan at the peninsula's tip Porte des Morts (literally Door of Death) after a large party of Indians was drowned in a sudden, fierce storm. Door County took the name when it was founded in 1851.

The peninsula has two distinct personalities. The Lake Michigan shore, exposed to ocean-like weather and crashing waves, is comparatively unsettled (it's sometimes called the "quiet side"). The relatively calm waters of Green Bay are a sailor's paradise, with a coastline dotted with sheltered coves and gleaming Victorian hamlets. Even the weather varies across the narrow peninsula, and a gray, fog-bound day along Lake Michigan's coast may be bright and sunny on the Green Bay shore.

The right combination of soil and climate provides an ideal environment for growing cherries and apples; orchards are found throughout Door County. At the peak of the harvest—cherries in August, apples in October—you can pick your own at many orchards or buy at roadside stands and farm markets.

In recent years, county residents have planted nearly a million daffodil bulbs. Add 7,000 acres of white cherry blossoms and pink apple blossoms and uncounted acres of wildflowers, and the peninsula in spring is awash with color. The entire county celebrates with a two-week-long Festival of Blossoms, beginning the second week in May.

Door County's sparkling seascapes and rugged scenic beauty have drawn large numbers of artists and craftspeople to the peninsula. Galleries abound, and some artists welcome visitors to their studios. Nationally acclaimed theater groups and music festivals also call the peninsula home.

No trip to Door County would be complete without experiencing a Door County fish boil. Handed down by the Scandinavians who settled the peninsula, the meal consists of red potatoes, onions, and fresh whitefish steaks, all placed in a huge cauldron and brought to a boil over a wood fire. At the moment the fish is cooked to perfection, kerosene is dumped on the fire, causing it to erupt in a roaring, fiery boil over. The steaming whitefish and vegetables are served with melted butter, cole slaw, and another Door County favorite, cherry pie. You'll have no trouble finding fish boils—they're available in virtually every village on the peninsula.

Door County is "more" country—more miles of coastline (250), more lighthouses (a dozen), and more state parks (five) than any other county in the United States. Between mid-June and mid-October, about two million people visit each year. While even the smallest shoreside hamlet offers a wide array of accommodations—condos, cabins, resorts, motels, rental homes, campgrounds—this is not the place to come without reservations.

Two major roads lead into the peninsula—State Highway 57, running northeast from Green Bay (the city), and State Highway 42, which follows Lake Michigan's shore north from Two Rivers. They merge a few miles south of Sturgeon Bay, the county seat and largest city on the peninsula.

No matter where in the county you're bound, stop first at the Door County Chamber of Commerce Information Center (State Highway 42/57 at the south edge of Sturgeon Bay) for maps, brochures, and information on every facet of Door County travel.

Sturgeon Bay turned from lumbering to shipbuilding in 1891 with the completion of a canal across the peninsula that linked Green Bay and Lake Michigan. Running east-west through the heart of the city, the partially man-made channel shortened the  water route from Green Bay to Milwaukee or Chicago by 100 miles and eliminated the dangerous Porte des Morts passage.

In the heyday of shipbuilding, Sturgeon Bay yards turned out fishing boats, car ferries (the SS *Badger* was built here; see Chapter 8), naval vessels including wooden minesweepers, and Great Lakes freighters. Lake freighters still lay up here in winter, and naval ships, commercial vessels, and luxury yachts are built for worldwide export.

State Highway 42/57 loops along the south and east edge of downtown Sturgeon Bay, crossing the ship canal on the new Bayview Bridge, then heads up the peninsula. Save the bypass for the return trip. Exit at Business 42/57 (Green Bay Road), and wind down the hill to the ship canal.

Here, you'll find the Door County Maritime Museum (Madison Avenue and Michigan Street), featuring exhibits of local maritime history, including boats from the early 1900s. As you approach the bridge, look to the right for the Coast Guard cutter that's stationed here. Guided tours are available when the vessel is in port. As you cross the ship canal on the "old" bridge, the boatyard on the right is Palmer Johnson, which specializes in custom racing craft and luxury yachts for worldwide export. The big shipyard off to the left is Bay Shipbuilding, where several thousand-foot-long Great Lakes freighters were constructed in the 1970s and early 1980s.

The Door County Museum (Fourth Avenue and Michigan Street) exhibits an eclectic collection of historical artifacts from the 1850s, including early fire-fighting equipment. Nearby, the noted Miller Art Center, in the Door County Library, features a permanent collection of 20th-century

Wisconsin and Midwest art, changing exhibits, and a performing-arts series.

The big, rambling Victorian homes built with lumbering and shipbuilding money in the late 19th and early 20th centuries provide inn and bed-and-breakfast aficionados a wide range of choices, from the 14-room White Lace Inn to the Inn at Cedar Crossing, featuring Victorian guest rooms and a popular restaurant specializing in regional cuisine.

Potawatomi State Park, located along the south side of the ship canal (follow the signs from State Highway 42/57), features two miles of Green Bay shoreline and the only downhill ski slope in Door County. Wisconsin's Ice Age Trail, which follows the glacial landscape across the state for 1,000 miles, begins (or ends) here. There are hiking and biking trails, wooded campsites, and an observation tower that provides spectacular views of Green Bay.

The lighthouse at the Ship Canal Coast Guard Station has marked the canal's Lake Michigan entrance since 1899. A parking lot at the station lets you get close enough for photos. To reach it, exit State Highway 42/57 onto Utah Street just north of the Bayview Bridge, turn right onto Cove Road, then left on Canal Road, which leads to the station.

State Highways 42 and 57 go their separate ways a couple of miles north of Sturgeon Bay, with State Highway 42 making for the Green Bay shore and State Highway 57 setting off toward Lake Michigan.

Turn right and follow State Highway 57 as it angles northeastward past a patchwork of farms and woods and through the communities of Institute and Valmy. Take the time to visit Whitefish Dunes State Park (turn right on County WD just north of Valmy and go east four miles). The day-use-only park (no camping) was created to preserve a fragile lakeshore environment that includes the highest sand dunes on the western shore of Lake Michigan (93 feet) and rare and threatened plants, such as dune goldenrod and dwarf lake iris. The long sand beach is ideal for sunbathing and beachcombing (Lake Michigan waters are very cold for swimming), and there are hiking trails among the dunes.

Next door is Cave Point, a small county park within the state park (a half mile down a gravel road from Whitefish Dunes; a sign points out the way). Here, Lake Michigan waves have hollowed out caves in the shoreline limestone, and you can hear water gurgling far beneath your feet as you stroll the rocky ledges along the water's edge. On a windy day, when big waves crash into the caves, the ground actually trembles. There's a small, shady picnic area overlooking the lake.

Back to State Highway 57 and northward. The road slices through woods and by an occasional stone-fenced farm field, finally fetching up on the Lake Michigan shore at Jacksonport. A mile north of town, tiny Meridian Park marks the 45th parallel. Here, you're exactly halfway between the Equator and the North Pole.

With glimpses of Lake Michigan through the trees and between the pricey homes that are rapidly taking root, State Highway 57 quietly works its way northward to Baileys Harbor (seven miles). Founded by commercial fishermen in 1851, Baileys Harbor is the oldest village in the county and a hot spot for Lake Michigan charter-boat fishing (brown trout, chinook salmon, or steelhead, depending on the time of year). Fishing or no, Gordon Lodge and the Baileys Harbor Yacht Club & Resort offer two good reasons to spend some time here.

The Ridges Sanctuary, a privately held, 900-acre wildflower preserve at the north edge of town, is home to all 28 species of orchids native to Wisconsin, along with other native-plant communities. There are hiking trails and a small nature center. Within the reserve are two historic range lights built in 1869 (no longer in service) that marked the channel into Baileys Harbor for a century.

If you like lighthouses, it's time for a detour. Follow County Q past the Ridges and around Moonlight Bay to Cana

Baileys Harbor scene

Island Road, and turn right to reach Cana Island Lighthouse, one of the most photographed and painted spots in the county.

A speck of land lying a quarter mile offshore, Cana Island is connected to the mainland by a low, rocky causeway (usually wet, a pair of old tennies may be in order). The lighthouse was built in 1869, and its automated beacon remains in service, warning ships away from dangerous reefs and shoal waters. The grounds are open daily between 10:00 A.M. and 5:00 P.M. (the buildings are closed to visitors). Check the white wooden box beside the path at the west edge of the grounds for historical information and a guest register.

Hard to imagine while you're snapping pictures on a sunny day, but a storm in October 1880 sent 10-foot waves pounding against the light keeper's quarters, with spray breaking near the top of the light tower. Dozens of sailing vessels were wrecked on peninsula shores, including seven at Baileys Harbor. According to newspaper accounts of the day, the light remained in service throughout, but the light keeper and his family were forced to flee to a boathouse on slightly higher ground. They came through unscathed, but high waters drowned the keeper's chickens.

Back on the mainland (and in dry shoes), you're given two choices: retrace your steps to Baileys Harbor, and turn north on State Highway 57, or head north on County Q. The Baileys Harbor/State Highway 57 route leads through maple forests and past stone-fenced fields and orchards; County Q meanders along the shores of North Bay before heading west across the peninsula interior to join State Highway 57. In either case, we're headed north to Sister Bay.

Sister Bay, with a population of 695, is the largest community in northern Door County. The annual Fall Festival, held in mid-October, is the county's largest celebration, bar none.

Like other towns along the Green Bay coast, Sister Bay is long and narrow, wrapped around a sparkling cove at the base of the wooded bluffs and headlands that dominate the western shore. There's a fine sand beach downtown, with a waterfront park and a marina filled with gleaming sailboats and power yachts.

Yes, those really are goats grazing on the grassy roof of Al Johnson's Swedish Restaurant. The lines here are sometimes long, but Swedish pancakes served with lingonberries and ice cream (yes!) will jump-start your day. Fish boils are available at Little Sister Resort (State Highway 42 to the south edge of town, then west on Little Sister Road).

Lots of shops, galleries, and studios are here, including Jack Anderson Art Gallery, known for traditional florals, landscapes, and still lifes.

Having done its duty, State Highway 57 ends here. State Highway 42 takes over, climbing steeply as it heads northward from Sister Bay. There are several orchards along the six-mile stretch to Ellison Bay. Seaquist Orchards Farm Market offers fresh-baked goods, jams, and jellies, as well as cherries, apples, strawberries, and raspberries in season.

The view of the Ellison Bay harbor from the escarpment at the south edge of the village is among the most picturesque seascapes in all of Wisconsin. Several potters call this village of 200 home, as does The Clearing, a school of the arts, literature, and ecological appreciation. The Viking Restaurant, downtown, features fish boils.

Turning inland as it leaves Ellison Bay, State Highway 42 loops east and north through maple forests to tiny Gills Rock, a commercial-fishing port at the tip of the peninsula.

Two passenger ferries to Washington Island depart from here (May through October) and are met at the Washington Island dock by trams offering narrated tours of the island. Or you can rent a moped or bicycle upon arrival. All-day parking in the Gills Rock municipal lot, a grassy field, costs $1.00. Payment is on the honor system.

If you've time before departure, peruse the commercial-fishing artifacts and items recovered from Death's Door shipwrecks at the local branch of the Door County Maritime Museum. You can also spend some time at the Top O' the Thumb Gift Shop (beautiful Norwegian sweaters) or stroll out on the jetty for a peek into a working, commercial-fishing tug.

If you wish to take your vehicle to the island, the Washington Island Ferry Line provides year-round auto and

passenger service. Ferries depart from
Northport Pier, two miles east of Gills
Rock at the end of State Highway 42.

Washington Island, which lies six
miles northeast of the peninsula and a 40-
minute ferry ride across Death's Door, is home
to about 650 people, predominantly Scandinavians,
who celebrate their heritage with a Scandinavian Festival on
the first weekend in August. A smattering of island fishermen
still wrest a living from the surrounding waters, mostly to provide whitefish for the peninsula's fish boils.

A billboard-style map near the harbor gives you an idea of
how the island is laid out. Stop at the Art and Nature Center,
in a former schoolhouse at Main and Jackson Harbor Roads
(take Main Road north from the harbor), to see watercolors,
prints, stained glass, and jewelry by local artists; nature hikes
and programs are also offered.

Two museums document the island's past and way of life.
The Washington Island Farm Museum (Jackson Harbor Road
at Airport Road) features pioneer buildings, farm tools, and
machinery. Jacobsen's Museum (take Main Road north to
Little Lake, and follow the signs) displays items of Native
American cultures, antiques, and rocks and fossils gathered
on the island.

But the real attractions here are solitude and scenery.
Farms and open fields dot the island, and deep forests provide
hiding places for deer and other woodland creatures. One hundred miles of roads make it easy to explore.

If you really seek solitude, head for Jackson Harbor, and
take the Rock Island passenger ferry to Rock Island State
Park, a 900-acre wilderness park lying a mile to the northeast. The *Karfi*, with a capacity of 46 passengers, makes regular trips in summer.

From 1910 until 1965, Rock Island was the private estate
of millionaire inventor Chester Thordarson. Several stone

buildings from the estate are now part of the park, including massive Viking Hall, which has park interpretive exhibits and original furnishings from the estate.

As a wilderness park, Rock Island is off limits to autos, bicycles, and other wheeled or motorized vehicles of any sort. Backpacker camping is permitted, and drinking water and firewood are available. Campers, hikers, and picnickers must bring all other supplies. Potawatomi Lighthouse, the oldest lighthouse on Lake Michigan, stands on the island's northwest corner (closed to visitors).

Back on the mainland, head south from Gills Rock on State Highway 42, and turn east (left) onto County NP for a short detour to Newport State Park. The park's 11 miles of Lake Michigan shoreline include long sandy beaches, hidden coves, and rocky headlands. Few visitors venture far beyond the beach at the picnic area, so it's not too difficult to find a private spot for beachcombing or sunning.

Return to State Highway 42, and backtrack south through Ellison Bay and Sister Bay to Ephraim (15 miles south of Gills Rock). Nestled along the shore of Eagle Harbor, the village was settled in 1853 by Moravians who came to the New World from Norway and has somehow managed to retain much of the Victorian charm that attracted the first tourists in the late 19th century. Fry Bal, a Scandinavian festival welcoming summer (bonfires on the beach at dusk, Norse ceremonies), is held in mid-June.

Elquist's Door County Market, at the north edge of town, has a great bakery and deli and sells fudge, smoked fish, and other Door County delights.

Downtown, buy an ice-cream cone and settle down to watch a spectacular sunset. Historic Anderson Dock, where early tourists arrived by coastal steamer, is home to the Peninsula Art Association's Hardy Gallery. A season-long show of work by county and regional artists and three changing invitational shows are presented each summer. Across the street, the Anderson Barn Museum has photos and artifacts from Ephraim's past.

A long list of resorts, inns, and motels provides equally as many reasons to dawdle a while. The French Country Inn began life in 1912 as a summer cottage for a large Chicago family with 10 children and is now a commodious bed-and-breakfast with a huge fireplace in the common room. The Hillside Hotel (1890), a restored European-style inn, offers bed-and-breakfast accommodations with feather beds and a private beach.

On the recommendation of a local resident, I had dinner at the Greenwood Supper Club, southeast of town on County A. It turned out to be one of those good northern Wisconsin steak houses that are a delight to discover.

Peninsula State Park, overlooking Green Bay from atop Eagle Bluff at the south edge of Ephraim, is one of Wisconsin's largest (3,763 acres) and most popular parks (one million plus visitors each year). Twenty miles of roads wind through the park; a map, available free at the park office, makes it much easier to find your way around.

Along with the typical park amenities—swimming beaches, a nature center, lakeview picnic areas, campgrounds (472 campsites), hiking trails, and biking roads—Peninsula has an 18-hole public golf course, the only golf course in a Wisconsin state park. American Folklore Theater's musical and historical presentations in the park amphitheater pack 'em in from early June to mid-August (performances are at the Fish Creek Town Hall from Labor Day to mid-October).

Also located within the park is Eagle Bluff Lighthouse, built in 1868 and still operating. It's the only lighthouse in the county open to visitors on a regular basis. Guided tours, excluding the light tower, are offered daily from early June to mid-October.

If you enter Peninsula's north entrance at Ephraim and exit the south entrance at Fish Creek, you've bypassed a five-mile stretch of State Highway 42. And you've missed a magnificent piece of 1950s memorabilia—the Skyway Drive-In Theater, one of the few left in the state (double features on weekends in May, nightly June through Labor Day).

Fish Creek, once a port that sold cordwood for fuel to Great Lakes steamers, is now the bustling southern gateway to Peninsula State Park. As home to the Peninsula Players (oldest summer theater in America), the Peninsula Music Festival (August), and the Peninsula Art School, the village lays fair claim to the title of peninsula arts center.

Lots of shops here, with handcrafted jewelry, fiber arts, fudge, leather goods, T-shirts, and the occasional rubber tomahawk. Fish Creek Kite Company advertises "serious kites just for fun." At Edgewood Orchards Gallery (Peninsula Player Road off State Highway 42 south), I saw a piece of art glass priced at $10,000. Hands in pockets, I settled for something a bit less pricey.

Fish Creek's White Gull Inn was established in 1896. Fish boils, complete with live accordion music while the fish are cooking, are served year-round on selected evenings. The dining rooms are Door County classic, with big stone fireplaces and lots of pine paneling. Lodging is available in both individual rooms and cottages.

Up the hill and heading south, State Highway 42 glides past Ray's Cherry Hut (fresh fruit in season, smoked salmon, jellies and jams, cheese, sausage, maple syrup) and through Juddville (don't blink) into quaint Egg Harbor.

Two tales circulate about the village name. One says an early settler named it for a nest of duck eggs. The other claims the name results from an 1825 conflict between the crews of two boats that entered the harbor at the same time. Each tried to reach shore first, and when one boat pulled ahead, the crew of the other pelted it with eggs.

Be that as it may, the village's deep, sheltered harbor is popular with boaters and fishermen. In summer (mid-June through mid-August), the renowned Birch Creek Music Festival draws big crowds to its jazz, ragtime, and big-band concerts.

The Village Cafe, a local favorite, has fresh-baked goods, homemade soups, and (you guessed it) traditional Door County fish boils. Egg Harbor offers some tony places to put up for the night, including the Egg Harbor Lodge (no children under 17), the plush Landmark Resort and Conference Center, and The Ashbrooke (French country suites).

Leaving Egg Harbor, State Highway 42 pulls away from the bay for the final time, passing the Olde Orchard Antique Mall (80 dealers) on the way out of town. In tiny Carlsville, the Door Peninsula Winery, occupying the old Carlsville schoolhouse, offers tours and tastings of its fruit wines.

Minutes later, State Highway 42 rejoins State Highway 57, and we're back in Sturgeon Bay. Our Door County sampler is complete.

For More Information

Door County Chamber of Commerce (Sturgeon Bay):
  920-743-4456 or 800-527-3529

Door County Maritime Museum (Sturgeon Bay): 920-743-5958

Door County Historical Museum (Sturgeon Bay): 920-743-5809

Miller Art Center (Sturgeon Bay): 920-746-0707

White Lace Inn (Sturgeon Bay): 920-743-1105

Inn at Cedar Crossing (Sturgeon Bay): 920-743-4200

Potawatomi State Park: 920-746-2890

Whitefish Dunes State Park: 920-823-2400

Gordon Lodge (Baileys Harbor): 920-839-2331

Baileys Harbor Yacht Club & Resort: 920-839-2336 or 800-927-2492

Ridges Sanctuary (Baileys Harbor): 920-839-2802

Al Johnson's Swedish Restaurant (Sister Bay): 920-854-2626

Little Sister Resort (Sister Bay): 920-854-4013

Jack Anderson Art Gallery (Sister Bay): 920-854-5161

The Clearing (Ellison Bay): 920-854-4088

Viking Restaurant (Ellison Bay): 920-854-2998

Door County Maritime Museum (Gills Rock): 920-743-5958

Washington Island Ferry Line: 920-847-2546

Washington Island Chamber of Commerce: 920-847-2179

Art and Nature Center (Washington Island): 920-847-2025

Washington Island Farm Museum: 920-847-2156 or 920-847-2032

Jacobsen's Museum (Washington Island): 920-847-2213

Rock Island Ferry (Washington Island): 920-847-2252

Rock Island State Park: 920-847-2235

Newport State Park: 920-854-2500

French Country Inn (Ephraim): 920-854-4001

Hillside Hotel (Ephraim): 920-854-2417 or 800-423-7023

Greenwood Supper Club (Fish Creek): 920-839-2451

Peninsula State Park: 920-868-3258

American Folklore Theater (Fish Creek): 920-839-2329

Skyway Drive-In Theater (Ephraim): 920-854-9938

Peninsula Players Theater (Fish Creek): 920-868-3287

Peninsula Music Festival (Fish Creek): 920-854-4060

Peninsula Art School (Fish Creek): 920-868-3455

Edgewood Orchards Gallery (Fish Creek): 920-868-3579

White Gull Inn (Fish Creek): 920-868-3517

Birch Creek Music Festival (Egg Harbor): 920-868-3763

Village Cafe (Egg Harbor): 920-868-3342

Egg Harbor Lodge: 920-868-3215

Landmark Resort and Conference Center (Egg Harbor): 920-868-3205

The Ashbrooke (Egg Harbor): 920-868-3113

Door Peninsula Winery (Carlsville): 920-743-7431

10

Northern Lakes and Woods Country

Getting there: From Chicago (approximately 330 miles), take I-90 northwest to State Highway 78 at Portage. From there, follow the signs to U.S. Route 51, and take it north to Merrill. Then follow State Highway 17 northeast through Rhinelander to Eagle River.

From Milwaukee (approximately 190 miles), take I-94 west to Madison, then follow I-94 northwest to State Highway 78 at Portage, and follow the signs to U.S. Route 51. Take it north to Merrill, and then follow State Highway 17 northeast through Rhinelander to Eagle River.

Highlights: North woods lake scenery and resort towns to explore; Eagle River with Carl's Wood Art Museum; Sayner with the Vilas County Museum; Woodruff–Minocqua and the Dr. Kate Museum, Sheer's Lumberjack Show, the Circle M Corral, and Jim Peck's Wildwood; Hazelhurst with the Northern Lights Playhouse and Wilderness Cruises. Allow a weekend.

A large portion of Wisconsin's northern lakes and woods country lies within Vilas and Oneida Counties. Together, these two counties have a combined total of more than 900 named lakes, with another 1,600 or so that no one has gotten around to naming. The chain of 28 lakes connected by the Eagle River, in Vilas County, is said to be the largest chain of inland lakes in the world.

More than half of Wisconsin's muskie lakes are found in Vilas and Oneida Counties, so it's not too difficult to see what direction recreation takes. Some of the best muskie fishing in the world is found here, and there is excellent fishing for walleye, northern pike, largemouth and smallmouth bass, as well as several species of panfish. In this neck of the woods, the word "fishing" rolls off the tongue in *italics*.

Snowmobiling takes over in winter (the snowmobile was invented in Vilas County), and the two counties offer riders more than 1,000 miles of interconnected trails.

Nestled between the 661,000-acre Nicolet National Forest and the 220,000-acre Northern Highland–American Legion State Forest, Eagle River, the county seat of Vilas County, is the hands-down "Snowmobile Capital of the World." Each winter, the community hosts two of the most prestigious snowmobile races in the world. The World Championship Snowmobile Derby, held the third weekend in January, features four days of high-speed action, run on a half-mile, high-banked, iced oval track. The Twenty-Four-Hour Enduro Race is held a week later. While it's not much to look at in summer, the track brings to Eagle River in January what auto racing brings to Indianapolis in May.

A former fur-trading outpost and logging center, Eagle River became the hub of a summer-resort industry as the logging era faded. The town's population of 1,400 swells tenfold or more in summer, and on rainy days, when campers come to town, traffic is extra heavy.

A stop at the Eagle River Information Center, located

downtown in a former railroad depot, provides a wealth of maps, brochures, and information about area attractions and accommodations. Where to stay? To spend just one night at each of the inns, bed-and-breakfasts, motels, mom-and-pop fishing camps, and tony resorts listed in the Eagle River area brochures would require nearly five months!

Carl's Wood Art Museum, at the south edge of town, is a treasure of north woods folk art. The museum features dozens of chainsaw carvings, including a 14-foot, 5,000-pound grizzly bear, a pair of giant cowboy boots, and a 25-foot wooden chain (each link weighs 30 pounds). Antique wood-carving tools, miniature carvings, and a fascinating collection of natural oddities, including translucent woods, burls, unusual tree trunks, and strange root configurations, round out the collection.

On the south shore of the Eagle River, in town, the Trees for Tomorrow Natural Resources Education Center has a self-guiding forest and wildlife demonstration trail.

When it's time to leave, head west on State Highway 70, which crosses the Eagle River at the edge of town, sliding along the lower end of Watersmeet Lake, where the Eagle and Wisconsin Rivers join briefly before going their separate ways.

Weaving slightly, here and there dancing over rocks and rapids, the Wisconsin River becomes our traveling companion and State Highway 70 weaves and dances in its company. Four miles farther along is Otter Rapids Dam, built in 1909 and the first of 26 hydroelectric plants on the Wisconsin River that convert the river's power to electricity.

As you continue westward, the pines and birches are joined by year-round homes, summer cottages, and a variety of commercial enterprises (go-cart track, riding stable, real estate offices, supper clubs, and roadhouses) that pop up along the way. Most crossroads sport a tall post covered with signs of the same exact size, shape, and style of lettering, each naming a resort hidden deep within the trees.

Deer Trail, Robin Drive, Sunset Road, and Cove Lane slide in from the north to join our westbound thoroughfare—was it the burly lumberjacks who chose such genteel names?

Just beyond Shady Lane, the Wisconsin River takes its leave, heading south for a rendezvous with the Mississippi. State Highway 70 continues westward into the huge Northern Highland–American Legion State Forest (fishing, canoeing, camping, with 18 family campgrounds, hiking, and lots of solitude). Then, with Little St. Germain Lake, South Bay, and West Bay on the right, the road eases into the village of St. Germain.

At the east edge of town, the International Snowmobile Racing Hall of Fame honors champions of the sport with displays of historic racing sleds and other racing memorabilia. Downtown, at the Chamber of Commerce Information Center, a tall statue of Chief St. Germaine (spelled with an "e") pays tribute to early Native Americans and a late 17th-century French soldier named François St. Germaine, who married a Chippewa Indian woman and settled here with his wife's people. Pick up maps and information on area attractions. Here, too, the list of lodging accommodations is varied—and long.

Across the road (just follow your nose!), the St. Germain Bake Shoppe offers made-from-scratch delights that send taste buds into ecstasy (open at 6:30 A.M.). The Pub 'n Prime, Whitetail Inn, and Clearview Supper Club provide three good reasons to stick around for dinner. Weekly family fishing seminars (summer), a bang-up July 4th celebration, and the annual autumn Colorama Celebration (September) top St. Germain's calendar of events.

At the west edge of town, take State Highway 155 north past Big St. Germain Lake and Lost Lake (Found Lake is close by) to the village of Sayner (seven miles). Here, in 1924, local resident Carl Eliason developed the prototype of the modern snowmobile. Eliason's machine, essentially a long toboggan powered by a small gasoline engine, steered with skis under the front and driven by an endless track mounted at the rear, played a major role in making north woods tourism a year-round proposition. You can see that original machine, along with other vintage snowmobiles, at Sayner's Vilas County Museum. Other exhibits document the region's natural history, logging industry, and Native American heritage (open Memorial Day through late September).

In summer, the Plum Ski-Ters present water-ski show excitement on Tuesday, Thursday, and Sunday evenings at nearby Plum Lake.

Backtrack a bit on State Highway 155, then follow County C south along the west shore of Big St. Germain Lake to State Highway 70, and turn west (right). A few miles along the way, our country road crosses a narrow strip of land dividing Little Arbor Vitae Lake from Big Arbor Vitae Lake and skirts the south edge of the village of Arbor Vitae. Two miles later, it joins U.S. Route 51 and turns south into the twin resort communities of Woodruff and Minocqua.

Close as two peas in a pod, it's hard to tell where one town ends and the other begins, although Minocqua's population is twice that of Woodruff. Born as late 19th-century logging settlements, both communities turned to tourism when the logging industry faded. Stoplights, national fast-food chains, and upscale shops and galleries belie a combined population of 5,400. Here, too, the lodging accommodations are many and varied; more than three months would be required to stay one night at each listing in the Minocqua–Woodruff–Arbor Vitae lodging guide.

Sheer's Lumberjack Show, in downtown Woodruff, keeps the region's logging heritage alive with log rolling, chopping and sawing, speed climbing, and other lumberjack skills and entertainments.

Woodruff is also home of the Dr. Kate Museum, preserving the memory of a pioneer country doctor who reached her patients on snowshoes when winter snows made roads impassable. Dr. Newcomb was the subject of a 1954 telecast of Ralph Edwards's *This Is Your Life* and a bestselling biography, *Dr. Kate, Angel on Snowshoes*. Museum exhibits include a replica of her office and displays about the region's logging, railroading, and farming days.

Many Woodruff/Minocqua attractions have wildlife themes. To see prized game fish in their infancy, visit the Woodruff State Fish Hatchery, one of the world's largest coolwater hatcheries and producers of muskies, northern pike, and walleye. The popular Jim Peck's Wildwood, located just west of Minocqua on State Highway 70, features more than 100 varieties of tame wildlife; you can pet a porcupine or a llama, feed tame deer, and see bear and hundreds of other animals in a north woods setting.

There's fishing, of course. And Minocqua lies at one end of the 18-mile-long Bearskin State Trail, a hiking/biking/snowmobiling trail that follows a former railroad bed through the scenic lakes country. Alert (and quiet) hikers and bikers might see an eagle or osprey.

But lest you feel you've strayed too deep into the piney woods, fear not—the Circle M Corral offers kiddie rides, go-carts, bumper boats, and train rides.

At mealtime, Bosacki's Boathouse is a longtime Minocqua favorite. The prodigious meals at Paul Bunyan's Lumberjack Cook Shanty (U.S. Route 51 between Woodruff and Minocqua) include camp breakfasts and lumberjack luncheons and dinners.

Hazelhurst, a few miles south on U.S. Route 51, is home to the Northern Lights Playhouse, where professional actors present dramas, musicals, and comedies, including Broadway hits; a children's theater is also offered. You can peek into the backcountry surrounding the Willow Reservoir on a sight-seeing, brunch, or dinner cruise offered by Wilderness Cruises. The scenery is lovely anytime and absolutely spectacular during the autumn-color season.

When it's time to go, U.S. Route 51 leads south to Madison and the interstates for Chicago and Milwaukee.

For More Information

Eagle River Information Center: 715-479-8575 or 800-359-6315

World Championship Snowmobile Derby (Eagle River): 715-479-4424 or 715-479-2764

Carl's Wood Art Museum (Eagle River): 715-479-1883

Trees for Tomorrow Natural Resources Education Center (Eagle River): 715-479-6456

Northern Highland–American Legion State Forest: 715-356-5211

International Snowmobile Racing Hall of Fame (St. Germain): 715-479-5466

St. Germain Chamber of Commerce: 800-727-7203

St. Germain Bake Shoppe: 715-479-9188

Pub 'n Prime (St. Germain): 715-479-7331

Whitetail Inn (St. Germain): 715-542-2541

Clearview Supper Club (St. Germain): 715-542-3865

Vilas County Museum (Sayner): 715-542-3388

Minocqua–Arbor Vitae–Woodruff Area Chamber of Commerce (Minocqua): 715-356-5266 or 800-446-6784

Sheer's Lumberjack Show (Woodruff): 715-356-4050 or 715-634-5010

Dr. Kate Museum (Woodruff): 715-356-6896

Woodruff State Fish Hatchery: 715-356-5211

Jim Peck's Wildwood (Minocqua): 715-356-5588

Bearskin State Trail (Minocqua): 715-385-2727

Circle M Corral (Minocqua): 715-356-4441

Bosacki's Boathouse (Minocqua): 715-356-5292

Northern Lights Playhouse (Hazelhurst): 715-356-7173

Wilderness Cruises (Hazelhurst): 715-453-3310 or 800-472-1516

11

Hurley, Hayward, and Hell

Getting there: To Hurley from Chicago (approximately 400 miles), take I-90 northwest to State Highway 78 at Portage. From there, follow signs to U.S. Route 51, and take that north to Hurley.

To Hurley from Milwaukee (approximately 305 miles), take I-94 west to Madison, follow I-90/94 northwest to State Highway 78 at Portage, follow signs to U.S. Route 51, and take it north to Hurley.

To Hurley from Minneapolis–St. Paul (approximately 225 miles), take I-94 east to Eau Claire, and follow U.S. Route 53 north to Chippewa Falls. Follow State Highway 29 east to Wausau, and take U.S. Route 51 north to Hurley.

To Hayward from Chicago or Milwaukee, take I-90/94 northwest to Eau Claire, follow U.S. Route 53 north to Trego, and take U.S. Route 63 northeast to Hayward. Hayward is 415 miles from Chicago, 340 miles from Milwaukee.

To Hayward from Minneapolis–St. Paul, take I-94 east to Eau Claire, then follow U.S. Route 53 north to Trego, and take U.S. Route 63 northeast to Hayward. Hayward is 140 miles from the Twin Cities.

Highlights: North woods scenery, historic mining towns, and picturesque waterfalls; Hurley with the Iron County Historical

Museum; Hayward, Sheer's Lumberjack Show, the National Freshwater Fishing Hall of Fame, and the Chippewa Flowage.

The seat of Iron County, Hurley lies in far northern Wisconsin, on the border with Michigan, in the heart of the famed Gogebic Iron Range, which stretches for 80 miles from Lake Gogebic in Michigan to Namekagon Lake in Wisconsin. Between the mid-1880s and mid-1960s, the Gogebic Range in Wisconsin produced 70 million tons of iron ore, more than half of which came from Hurley mines.

Iron County's natural resources also included a vast white pine forest, which produced the billions of board feet of lumber to build a growing Midwest. One lumbering firm, the Montreal River Lumber Company, alone milled 80,000 board feet of white pine a day, every day, between 1884 and 1904.

In its heyday, Hurley was a bawdy, boisterous boomtown with a population of 7,000 and more than happy to provide work-weary miners and lumberjacks (and later, deer hunters) with an evening's entertainment. Saloons (90 at the peak), gambling houses, and "variety clubs" (upstairs "sleeping" rooms, short-term rental) stood shoulder to shoulder on Silver Street. Perhaps because it catered to both miners and lumberjacks, Hurley gained a reputation as the most notorious "sin city" on the iron range. Its reputation was immortalized in Edna Ferber's novel *Come and Get It.*

Hurley, Hayward (its sister city in sin at the far western end of the Gogebic Range), and Hell were regarded as the three meanest, roughest places in the then-known universe.

The last iron mine closed more than 30 years ago. Hurley's population has dwindled to less than 2,000, and its checkered past is now part of folklore (mostly). Silver Street today is a favorite dining area with travelers.

Stop at the Iron County Historical Museum, located in the old county courthouse, to see exhibits recalling mining, logging, and other aspects of Hurley's rough-and-tumble days. The three-story, red-brick Victorian structure, complete with five-story clock tower, was built in 1892 as a town hall and became a courthouse with the creation of Iron County, in 1893. You can see the original clock works, still in operation, and, on most days, watch rug-weaving demonstrations at the museum.

Nature also blessed the Hurley area with many beautiful waterfalls, including some of the highest and most spectacular in Wisconsin. We'll visit eight easily reached waterfalls, six in Iron County and two in adjoining Ashland County. Begin with a stop at the Wisconsin Travel Information Center on U.S. Route 51 at the north edge of town, for a map with detailed directions to area falls.

Peterson Falls, on the East Branch of the Montreal River, is first on the list. Starting at the U.S. Route 2/51 overpass at the north edge of Hurley, head west on U.S. Route 2 for a half mile, and turn right on the unpaved road at the Ero Nasi Construction Company sign. Go straight ahead (past the turnoffs leading to the construction company and a stone quarry) for three-tenths of a mile to a small grassy turnaround. You can hear the falls roaring as soon as you step from the car. A footpath at the north edge of the turnaround leads to the 35-foot-high, pine-shrouded falls, half of which lies in Michigan.

The next stop is at Kimball Park Falls. Backtrack to U.S. Route 2, and head west for two and a half miles to Park Road, turn south (left), and travel for two-tenths of a mile to Town Park Road, then turn right, and follow the gravel road west a half mile to Kimball Town Park. This small, but pretty, waterfall on the West Branch of the Montreal River drops about 10 feet in a series of sparkling cascades above and below the bridge at the park entrance.

Return to Hurley and the four-way stop downtown at Silver Street. Turn west (right), and follow State Highway 77 west to Montreal (you're barely clear of Hurley before the road ambles into the outskirts of Montreal). Watch for a large brown-and-yellow sign on the right pointing to Gile and the Gile Flowage, and turn left onto Nimikon Street at the ballpark. Travel one block, turn right onto Kogagan Street, go down the hill for 50 yards to the intersection with Mellen Street, and, as Kogagan Street curves right, pull into the gravel parking area at the head of the marked snowmobile trail.

Gile Falls, on the West Branch of the Montreal River, is an easy two-minute walk along the gravel lane to the left. Keep an eye peeled—if there have not been many visitors, a great blue heron or pair of ducks may take flight at your intrusion. A scenic overlook offers a close view of the picturesque, 15-foot falls (it looks higher), set against vast piles of mine tailings (waste rock) from the Montreal Mine No. 5. A small snowmobile bridge crossing over the top of the falls is easily reached by following the gravel trail to the left of the overlook.

Back on State Highway 77 and continuing west, the road runs downhill into the heart of Montreal, population 838. Combining the 19th-century villages of Montreal and Gile, Montreal is a planned mining company town that was incorporated in 1924 and is today listed on the National Register of Historic Places. Gile, on the West Branch of the Montreal, was the center of the area's timber industries and home to the Montreal River Lumber Company. Montreal, on the hill, was the site of the Montreal Mining Company, which shipped more than 45 million tons of iron ore between 1886 and 1962. At its closing, the Montreal mine had reached a vertical depth of 4,335 feet.

Hurrying across the river, State Highway 77 leaves Montreal, climbing a hill past a mountain of mine tailings towering above Montreal's city hall, fire department, and library (all one building). On the left is a huge fieldstone building that formerly held the Montreal mine machine shop; to the right, a collection of small, nearly identical white frame houses that were company-built miners' homes.

Running southwesterly along the wooded Gogebic Range, State Highway 77 slips through Pence, once home to the Plummer Mine (there are more than 20 log buildings in the hamlet), and Iron Belt, named after a mine and now the gateway to the Whitecap Mountain Ski Area.

At the village of Upson, 12 miles from Hurley, turn north (right) onto State Highway 122, go three blocks to Upson Park Road, and turn left across the bridge to Upson Town Park. Here, the tree-lined Potato River makes a 19-foot plunge over Upson Falls. Not as well known as other Iron County waterfalls (a secret waterfall?), Upson Falls is lovely, especially during times of higher water. You can get an overview from the bridge, but a short, rocky path along the riverbank provides greater scenic rewards (well worth the effort). There are picnic tables and grills in the park.

Backtrack to State Highway 122, and continue northward. Crossing Alder Creek (almost big enough to be called a river), our country road plunges into a forest of poplar, pine, and birch, winding and climbing into the hills of the Gogebic Range. Logging roads make muddy slashes through the trees; pulpwood logs are piled within easy reach of the pavement. Marsh marigolds and cattails bloom in the low, spotty wetlands along the road. In spring, trilliums carpet the rugged forest floor. The deer I expected to see didn't materialize, but the occasional fire number at the head of a rocky dirt road indicates there is life within the forest. (A fire number, mounted on a post at a farmyard entrance, identifies that property within the local fire district. The number would be used to report a fire at that location.)

It is 10 miles from the village of Upson to the village of Saxon, but it seems much farther. I suddenly wondered if the spare tire still held air. Then, easing over the crest of a long, high hill, Lake Superior burst into view, a brilliant patch of blue on the horizon (as it turns out, 12 miles away). A long, twisty way down the hill and State Highway 122 swings into Saxon, leaving just as quickly to climb a hill to the intersection with U.S. Route 2.

Beyond the intersection, State Highway 122 gradually winds downhill toward the big lake, passing a cluster of dairy farms and the Saxon Harbor Berry Farm (strawberries in season) before the trees close in. Four miles from U.S. Route 2, State Highway 122 (and Wisconsin) ends at the Montreal River, the border with Michigan. Cross the bridge into Michigan, go a half mile east to the second driveway on the left (unmarked), and turn into the parking lot at the Superior Falls Hydro Station. Follow the sign and pathway a short distance west to the falls.

Hydro station aside, this is a lovely spot. In its final rush to Lake Superior, the Montreal River, with both branches now joined, crashes 90 feet over Superior Falls, which is among the most spectacular of Iron County's waterfalls. The view is from the top of the river gorge. Note that midmorning is the best time for photographs.

A short trail that starts on the east side of the hydro station leads to a scenic overlook of Lake Superior; the Bayfield Peninsula and Apostle Islands lie on the far horizon (see Chapter 12). There's also a canoe access trail (steep) leading down to the river and the gravel bar built up at the river's mouth. A patchwork of short, choppy waves marks the collision of river and lake.

Backtrack to Wisconsin and State Highway 122. Just west of the state line, a one-mile detour down County A leads to Saxon Harbor, a small-boat harbor of refuge and home port to several charter fishing boats. The settlement has a marina, a house or two, a cluster of summer cottages, and the Harbor Lights (cozy rainy-afternoon pub).

Return to U.S. Route 2, and turn west (right). There's a terrific view of Lake Superior from a wayside just beyond the intersection. Four miles farther along this busy, tree-lined highway, turn left onto State Highway 169, heading south past the North Woods Chapel (made of logs). The forest here is less dense than a few miles east, making room for a few small farms, summer cottages, and year-round homes with newly mown lawns.

Three miles along the way, State Highway 169 wanders down a steep hill into tiny Gurney. At the south edge of the village, watch for a sign pointing to the Potato River Falls. Turn west (right), and follow the gravel road for a mile and a half to the town park. Here, the Potato River drops about 90 feet over three great cataracts, the upper, middle, and lower falls of the Potato River.

The view is from the top of the river gorge. It's not a good idea to attempt to climb down to the falls as the eroded slopes of the gorge are steep and dangerous. A footpath at the northwest corner of the parking area leads to an overlook of the lower falls. You can see the middle and upper falls by following the footpaths south along the edge of the woods.

Back on State Highway 169 and heading south, our country road crosses the Potato River and continues on through the trees. More marsh marigolds in the wet spots, more trilliums, more homes and summer cottages.

Entering Ashland County, the road smooths out but becomes more winding and twisty. There are lovely views of the hills in the iron range and occasional large farms here, with silos and cattle grazing in lush green fields. Thirteen miles southwest of Gurney is Copper Falls State Park.

Copper Falls is what nonresidents picture a north woods Wisconsin state park to be—pines and hardwoods, wildflowers (thousands and thousands of trilliums in spring), log buildings, shady green picnic areas, a rushing river. In this case, add two roaring waterfalls, the eighth and ninth highest in the state.

Winding through the park on its rush northward to Lake Superior, the Bad River plunges 29 feet over the twin-pronged Copper Falls, then crashes through a deep gorge rimmed by pines, ferns, and white cedars. About a half mile downstream, Tyler's Forks of the Bad River slides over a series of sparkling cascades (magnificent in themselves) before tumbling 30 feet over Brownstone Falls into the gorge. The two streams join below the falls and surge over a long series of rapids known as Devil's Gate.

Starting at the main picnic area, an easy walking trail crosses a footbridge over the Bad River and follows the edge of the river gorge to overlooks of Copper Falls (a quarter mile) and Brownstone Falls (a half mile). It's a couple of miles if you follow the trail loop back to the starting point. Scenic overlooks, woods, wildflowers, and placards describing park geology add to the enjoyment.

There are many reasons to linger—hiking trails, wooded campgrounds, pleasant picnic areas, an above-average gift shop. Copper Falls is not an easy place to bid farewell.

But we must. More country roads beckon.

Bustling Hayward, population 1,897, was born in the winter of 1882 to 1883, when A. J. Hayward built a sawmill on the Upper Namekagon River of northwestern Wisconsin. Within a year, Hayward's population leapt from zero to 1,000.

At the peak of the boom, Hayward was a rip-roaring lumber town and city of sin in its own right, boasting 13 saloons and five brothels—Old Lady Schutte's was said to be the class of the field. For entertainment, men fought for drinks in the saloons, and the loser bought for the house. When things were really rolling, there was a fight on every street corner in town.

But, by comparison with Hurley, Hayward's time of iniquity was relatively short-lived. Most of the big white pines on the Upper Namekagon were logged off within two decades of the community's founding, and the lumbering companies moved on (almost overnight in some instances), although logging on a lesser scale continued for many more years.

Hayward celebrates its logging heritage by hosting the annual Lumberjack World Championships (nationally televised) in late July. You can also see such lumberjack skills and entertainments as log rolling, chopping, sawing, and speed climbing at Sheer's Lumberjack Show (mid-June to late August).

Fishing, especially muskie fishing on the Chippewa Flowage, brings many to the Hayward area. The Moccasin Bar, on Main Street, displays Cal Johnson's 60 1/4-inch world-record muskie, which weighed in at 67 1/2 pounds.

But the biggest muskie you'll ever see (143 feet long!) is at the National Freshwater Fishing Hall of Fame, at the edge of town on the banks of the Namekagon. The fish-shaped structure and five other museum buildings contain thousands of fishing artifacts, including antique outboard motors, fish mounts, rods and reels, a world-record photo gallery, and many other curios from the world of sportfishing.

Leaving Hayward, follow County B east into the Hayward lakes country. Weaving through the second-growth forest, our country road curves around the blue waters of Round Lake (left) and Little Round Lake (right). Resort-oriented signs are at every crossroad—bait shops, watering holes, taxidermy establishments, real estate offices, supper clubs, a golf course, even a pizza parlor carved into the forest. Not the wild north woods (in any aspect) of early Hayward. Mud Lake and Callahan Lake pass by, busy with boats bearing hopeful fishermen.

Just past Reed Lake, turn south (right) on County CC, and enter the Lac Courte Oreilles (la-coud-a-RAY) Indian Reservation. Mind the road for deer. The plastic white-tailed one grazing on the lawn of a township garage turned its head as I drove by.

Down past Twin Bay Road and just beyond Glover Lake, the Chippewa Flowage pops into view, dazzling in the afternoon sun of a late spring day. Created by a dam across the Chippewa River, the 17,000-acre lake is a hotbed of muskie fishing (walleyes, too).

Cross the center of the lake on a bridge and causeway (food, lodging, boats for rent at Herman's Landing), then go past Pokegama Lake, where County CC turns west through this world of deep blue water and dark green pines. James Slough slides by on the right as the road crosses diminutive Blueberry Bay and hurries on to Blueberry Lake, where Blueberry Resort stands on the shore (what else could you name it?). Ditto for Tiger Musky Resort, off to the right on Tiger Musky Road.

Three miles along the way, back in the forest near the junction with County N, is The Hideout, a onetime north woods retreat of Prohibition crime boss "Scarface" Al Capone and now a popular restaurant. Guided tours include the main lodge with its massive, native-stone fireplace and many original furnishings; the limousine garage, remodeled into a bar and dining room; and other buildings on the 400-acre estate.

Now head west on County N, where the pines stand dark against the yellow-green of birch and poplar, to tiny, tiny Reserve, on the shore of Little Lac Courte Oreilles. Turn north (right) onto County E, past the Indian Mission of St. Francis Salanus (visitors welcome, bingo Saturday at 6:30 P.M.) and along the shore of Lac Courte Oreilles.

With a zig and a zag on and off County K at the tribal commercial center, County E heads west by northwest, skirting Grindstone Lake, winding and climbing along the populous shore of pretty Spring Lake.

A stone's throw down Williams Road is Petty Lake and Schonerwald Haus, once the hunting lodge and hideaway of

1930s and 1940s pinup artist George Petty, whose work was featured in calendars and men's magazines of that era (*Esquire, True*). A 1950 movie entitled *The Petty Girl* starred Robert Cummings as the artist and Joan Caulfield as the girl of his inspiration.

A few more twists and turns, and we're back to County B. Just west is Hayward, starting point of this segment of our north woods odyssey.

For More Information

Iron County Historical Museum (Hurley): 715-561-2244

Wisconsin Travel Information Center (Hurley): 715-561-5310

Copper Falls State Park: 715-274-5123

Hayward Area Chamber of Commerce: 715-634-8662 or 800-724-2992

Sheer's Lumberjack Show (Hayward): 715-634-5010

National Freshwater Fishing Hall of Fame (Hayward): 715-634-4440

The Hideout (Couderay): 715-945-2746

12

By the Shining Big-Sea Water

Getting there: From Chicago (approximately 465 miles), take I-90 northwest to Madison, and follow I-94 west to Eau Claire. Follow U.S. Route 53 north to Superior.

From Milwaukee (approximately 390 miles), take I-94 west to Eau Claire. Follow U.S. Route 53 north to Superior.

From Minneapolis–St. Paul (approximately 165 miles), take I-35 north to Duluth, then follow U.S. Route 53 south to Superior.

Highlights: Picturesque fishing villages, state parks, and waterfalls; Superior, the SS *Meteor* Museum, and the Fairlawn Mansion and Museum; Bayfield, Apostle Islands National Lakeshore, and Lake Superior Big Top Chautauqua; La Pointe with Big Bay State Park and the Madeline Island Historical Museum; Ashland and the Ashland Historical Museum. The driving distance is approximately 100 miles. Allow two days, minimum.

The starting point for this tour is Superior, at the far western end of Lake Superior. We'll be traveling most of Wisconsin's segment of the Lake Superior Circle Tour, which passes through Michigan, Wisconsin, Minnesota, and the province of Ontario, Canada, spanning 1,300 miles as it encircles the world's largest body of freshwater.

Superior's natural deep-water harbor, combined with that of adjacent Duluth, Minnesota, makes up the world's largest inland ocean port—2,342 miles from the Atlantic Ocean via the St. Lawrence Seaway. Ships of many nations make Duluth–Superior a port of call during the nine months of the year that the harbor is free of ice.

In the 1890s, Superior shipyards wrote a page in Great Lakes history when they produced 43 strange-looking freighters called "whalebacks." During World War II, local shipyards constructed a total of 81 vessels (mostly freighters) for the war effort. In May 1943, the Walter Butler Company, which employed 5,000 workers, launched five large cargo ships in a single day.

Shipyards, grain elevators, heavy industry, and some of the world's largest docks line the 28 miles of shoreline surrounding the Duluth–Superior harbor. While considerably less busy than it was a dozen or so years ago, the harbor remains a fascinating place.

Narrated boat tours of the huge harbor depart from Barker's Island, a man-made island connected to U.S. Route 2/53 east (also called Harbor View Parkway East) by the Barker's Island Causeway.

A Wisconsin Travel Information Center, located just west of the causeway on a frontage road along U.S. Route 2/53, offers maps, brochures, and information about area attractions.

Barker's Island is also home to the SS *Meteor* Museum. Sole survivor of the whalebacks, the *Meteor* was launched in 1896, barely a mile from her permanent Barker's Island moorings. Like others of her peculiar breed, she featured a rounded, cigar-shaped hull, a blunt nose shaped like a pig's snout, and turret-like cabins raised above the spar deck on pillars. After more than 60 years of Great Lakes service, the *Meteor* was retired and has been preserved as a museum.

Near the ship, amid a collection of souvenir shops and a miniature golf course, is a Seaman's Memorial dedicated to the crew of the ill-fated lakes freighter *Edmund Fitzgerald*.

The 729-foot *Fitzgerald* departed Superior early in the afternoon of November 9, 1975, bound for Cleveland with a cargo of taconite (concentrated iron ore) and a crew of 29. Caught up in a storm of hurricane proportions, she sank near the eastern end of the lake the following evening, taking all hands with her. The crew included men who made their homes in Superior and nearby communities in both Wisconsin and Minnesota; the vessel's loss was especially hard felt in the western Lake Superior region.

Opposite Barker's Island, the 42-room Fairlawn Mansion recalls days of Victorian splendor. Built in 1890 by Martin Pattison, an early lumber baron and mayor of Superior, the mansion is today a museum housing the collections of the Douglas County Historical Society. First-floor rooms have been restored to 19th-century elegance. Second and third floors feature museum exhibits about prehistoric and Native American cultures of the Lake Superior region, European immigration and settlement, and regional industry.

Before heading east from Superior, make a side trip to one of Wisconsin's loveliest state parks. From Fairlawn, follow U.S. Route 2 west a mile or so to State Highway 35, then turn south. Twelve miles south of Superior is Pattison State Park, named for the aforementioned Martin Pattison, who donated the parklands. Pattison (1,373 acres) offers all the things you'd expect in a north woods park—a cool, sparkling lake; large, wooded campsites; lush, green picnic areas; and interesting hiking trails. Not to mention 165-foot Big Manitou Falls, the highest waterfall in Wisconsin and the fourth highest east of the Rocky Mountains. Photo tip: The falls are best photographed in the afternoon.

Return to Superior and follow U.S. Route 2/53 east along the lakeshore to the edge of town, then turn left on Moccasin Mike Road (big sign, you can't miss it). Follow it a half mile to Wisconsin Point Road, and turn left, following it to the end of the four-mile-long sandbar that forms Superior's harbor. The point is forested with pine, birch, and maple and supports a vast array of bird life, especially during the spring and autumn migrations. There are many sandy beach areas here, but on a muggy day in mid-June, with thunder rumbling over the lake, the black flies were so thick and so vicious that it was impossible to leave the car.

At the end of Wisconsin Point is the Superior Entry, the only natural opening in the great sandbar, and the historic Wisconsin Point Lighthouse (now automated).

Retrace your steps to U.S. Route 2/53, and travel southeast until U.S. Route 2 and U.S. Route 53 divide (about five miles). Stay on U.S. Route 2 for a short distance to the exit at County U, then follow County U north a half mile to Amnicon Falls State Park.

The Amnicon River descends 180 feet in a two-mile race through this lovely park, dancing over cataracts and plunging over three waterfalls, each about 30 feet high. The park is small (825 acres), but it's a wonderful place to sit beside a sparkling waterfall, take in the fragrance of the pines, and let the rest of the world do whatever it's up to at the moment. There's a small campground, should you wish to spend the night.

From Amnicon Falls, continue north through the woods on County U for five miles to State Highway 13, and you're back on the Lake Superior Circle Tour. Turn east (right), and you'll soon come to an eight-bladed Finnish windmill that was built in 1906. In operation until 1926, the mill produced about

40 barrels of flour a day. It's listed in both the State and National Registers of Historic Places.

Continuing eastward, State Highway 13 runs through a forest of second-growth poplar, birch, and pine. Scattered farms—some neat and orderly, some hardscrabble—sport woodpiles of mountainous proportions, vital where seasonal snowfalls total 100 inches or more and Lake Superior breezes can produce windchills of 60 degrees below zero.

Our country road undulates as it moves along, rising and falling like the gentlest of waves on the big lake (just out of sight for the moment). In the low points, rivers and streams, stained root-beer-brown by tannin in the tamarack swamps through which they flow, slide beneath the road. The rivers—the Amnicon and the Poplar—sparkle and prance as they rush northward to Lake Superior. The creeks—Middle, Lake, Pearson, and others—move lazily, as if less eager to lose their identity to the big lake.

Entering the long and narrow Brule River State Forest (you can drive across its width in 10 minutes or less), State Highway 13 crosses the famed Bois Brule River, one of the best trout-fishing and canoeing rivers in the Midwest. Five presidents, Ulysses S. Grant, Grover Cleveland, Calvin Coolidge, Herbert Hoover, and Dwight Eisenhower, have fished its sparkling waters.

The north-flowing Bois Brule and the south-flowing St. Croix Rivers (the headwaters of the two are connected by a short portage) form the historic link between Lake Superior and the Mississippi River. Native Americans used the route for centuries before the first Europeans arrived. Frenchman Daniel Greysolon, sieur du Lhut, namesake of the city of Duluth, is credited with "discovering" the river in 1680. European explorers, fur traders, and missionaries traveled the water route for a century and a half afterward.

After crossing the Bois Brule, State Highway 13 swings abruptly northward. Lake Superior soon pops into view, blue and shimmering if the day is sunny, gray and foreboding if it is not. The "Gitche Gumee" of Henry Wadsworth Longfellow's classic poem, *The Song of Hiawatha*, Superior is as big as lakes get—350 miles long and 160 miles wide—a tad larger than the state of South Carolina. Cold, too, with an average temperature of 39 degrees . . . year-round!

There's a picnic area at the mouth of the Bois Brule (follow the gravel Brule River Road westward for four miles; it's marked by a sign along State Highway 13).

Now rambling eastward along the shore, with Minnesota still visible on the northern horizon, State Highway 13 leads to Port Wing (population 503), a onetime logging center and commercial-fishing port, where in 1903 Wisconsin's first consolidated school district was organized. City Park exhibits a replica of the covered wagon used as the state's first school bus, a mail sled that saw use from 1915 until 1931, and the bell tower from that first consolidated school.

Continuing eastward, the road hurries through the hamlet of Herbster, perched on the lakeshore at the mouth of the Cranberry River, and across three tiny brooks named Lost Creek No. 3, Lost Creek No. 2, and Lost Creek No. 1 (how does one lose a creek?) before arriving in Cornucopia, Wisconsin's northernmost community. Take time to snap a picture of beautiful, onion-domed St. Mary's Russian Orthodox Church, at the south end of the village. A handful of gift shops along the waterfront near the small marina make for fun browsing, and you can dip your toe in the lake at nearby Siskiwit Bay Parkway, which has a small picnic shelter and a sand beach. If you're ready to call it a day, the Village Inn offers food, spirits, and lodging.

As State Highway 13 climbs upward at the east edge of the village, make a half-mile detour south on Siskiwit Falls Road to visit tiny, charming Siskiwit Falls.

Heading east from "Cornie," the road leaves the lakeshore, cutting a swath through the forest as it loops across the top of the Bayfield Peninsula, rejoining the lake on the Red Cliff Indian Reservation, which hugs the peninsula's north shore. The reservation casino offers bingo and Las Vegas–style gaming. There's also a modern campground and a marina on the reservation.

Three miles south of the reservation is Bayfield, a commercial-fishing village and one of the most picturesque communities on the south shore of Lake Superior. The Apostle Islands lay just offshore at Bayfield's doorstep.

Nineteenth-century dollars earned from logging, brownstone quarrying, and commercial fishing built the rambling Victorian houses that today give Bayfield some enticing bed-and-breakfasts, including the Cooper Hill House; Baywood Place; Grunke's First Street Inn; and the Old Rittenhouse Inn, famous both for its accommodations and its gourmet dining. Plan to stay awhile.

Tradition says 17th-century French missionaries counted a dozen emerald islands in Chequamegon Bay and named them for the Twelve Apostles. There are, in fact, 22 islands, lying between 1 and 25 miles off the mainland and spread across two counties (Bayfield and Ashland) and 600 square miles of western Lake Superior. The smallest is 3 acres in size, the largest, 14,000 acres. Twenty-one islands and a 12-mile section of forested mainland make up the Apostle Islands National Lakeshore.

The Apostle Islands National Lakeshore Visitor Center, occupying a beautiful old brownstone that was once the Bayfield County Courthouse, has films, lighthouse exhibits, and information about the national lakeshore. Wilderness camping is permitted on most islands, and campers can arrange shuttle service with Apostle Islands Cruise Service. The line also offers a variety of sight-seeing cruises, some of which make brief island stops.

There's a seasonal lakeshore visitors center located at Sand Bay, 13 miles north of Bayfield via State Highway 13. Guided and self-guided tours of a 1920s and 1930s commercial-fishing operation are available.

In autumn, as Lake Superior begins to release heat absorbed from the summer sun, warm lake breezes (relative term) provide the mainland lakeshore with a growing season somewhat longer than is found a few short miles inland. More than a dozen orchards are clustered in the hills above Bayfield. Apples are the main crop, but pears, cherries, raspberries, and blueberries are also grown, and the making of jams, jellies, and cider is a thriving cottage industry. Stop at the Bayfield Chamber of Commerce for a map that lists directions to the orchards. The annual Apple Festival is held in early October.

Spend some time exploring Bayfield's colorful waterfront, with its gleaming sailboats and motor yachts. A cup of coffee and a window table at the Pier Restaurant, overlooking the dock and marina at the foot of Rittenhouse Avenue, is good preparation for a stroll along the breakwaters. Bayfield's commercial-fishing tugs depart in the wee hours of the morning and usually return at midafternoon, chugging into port under a cloud of wheeling, screeching gulls begging for a handout. Both fresh and smoked fish are sold at the commercial-fishing docks. Whitefish livers are a local delicacy (acquired taste); each restaurant has its own special recipe.

For many visitors, a side trip to Madeline Island is high on the agenda. Island ferries depart from docks at the foot of Washington Avenue in Bayfield from April to late December, depending on the spring thaw and winter freeze. Take your auto or RV (the ferries easily carry large motor coaches), or ride as a passenger, and stroll around the island village of La Pointe. The three-mile-long crossing takes about 20 minutes.

At 14,000 acres, Madeline Island is the largest of the Apostles and has been inhabited for more than three centuries. It is the only island in the Apostles not included in the National Lakeshore.

The island's original settlers were Ojibwa people (also called Chippewa) who named it "Monawaunakauning," meaning "home of the golden-breasted woodpecker." Flickers still abound. Permanent European settlement dates from 1792, but the first Frenchmen to explore western Lake Superior were here in the early 1600s—perhaps even before the Pilgrims reached Plymouth Rock. The Madeline Island Historical Museum, standing on the site where the American Fur Company trading post once stood (one block from the ferry landing), has exhibits that encompass more than 300 years of island history.

There are dining and lodging accommodations in the village, a few gift and craft shops, a marina, and a golf course designed by the famed Robert Trent Jones. Narrated island bus tours are offered from mid-June to Labor Day.

The island is heavily wooded and, away from La Pointe, somewhat isolated. Big Bay State Park (follow County H and Hagen Road five miles east of town) has long sand beaches, a family campground, and miles of hiking trails. Forty-five miles of roads circle the island. Most are paved, but it's rough riding in places.

Back on the mainland, check the evening's playbill at Bayfield's Lake Superior Big Top Chautauqua before you leave town. Family-oriented concerts, plays, lectures, and original musicals are presented, in the spirit of the old-time "tent shows," in a 750-seat tent at Mt. Ashwabay Ski Area, three miles south of town. Nationally known entertainers occasionally appear.

Heading south from Bayfield, State Highway 13 slides gently downhill along the pine-studded Chequamegon Bay shoreline. Keep a sharp watch on the right side of the road for a barn with a great Lake Superior mural—ore freighters, gulls, sunsets, rainbows, and more!

Soon after crossing the Onion River, you're in Washburn, the present Bayfield County seat. Stop at the U.S. Forest Service headquarters on State Highway 13 for information on hunting, fishing, camping, skiing, and other recreational activities in the nearby Chequamegon National Forest. Washburn has two lakeshore parks with campgrounds: Memorial Park, with (ahem) cable television hookups at all sites with electricity, and West End Park, which has a bubbling artesian well.

Twelve miles farther south, State Highway 13 rejoins U.S. Route 2 at Ashland, at the foot of Chequamegon Bay. The fur traders Pierre Esprit Radisson and Médard Chouart des Groseilliers wintered here in 1659. There's a tiny commemorative log cabin in Bayview Park, at the east edge of town.

Ashland has some choice Romanesque Revival, Richardson Romanesque, classical revival, and neoclassical architecture built during its heyday as a railroading, lumbering, and iron-ore shipping center. The Ashland Historical Museum, housed in the 23-room Wilmarth Mansion (circa 1869), has exhibits documenting Ashland's first 100 years.

The old Soo Line Ore Dock, on Water Street, reaches out into Chequamegon Bay for some 1,800 feet, a deserted monolith recalling Ashland's rich mining and shipping history. Another historic structure, the former Soo Line Railroad Depot, today houses eateries and shops.

Before you go, stroll on the boardwalk that meanders along the downtown lakefront. Should you linger too long, the Hotel Chequamegon, a new version of a 19th-century hostelry of the same name, has turn-of-the-century ambience and rooms with lake views.

For More Information

Wisconsin Travel Information Center (Superior): 715-392-1662

SS *Meteor* Museum (Superior): 715-392-5742

Fairlawn Mansion and Museum (Superior): 715-394-5712

Pattison State Park: 715-399-3111

Amnicon Falls State Park: 715-398-3000 (summer),
715-399-3111 (winter)

Village Inn (Cornucopia): 715-742-3941

Bayfield Chamber of Commerce: 715-779-3335 or
800-447-4094

Cooper Hill House (Bayfield): 715-779-5060

Baywood Place (Bayfield): 715-779-3690 or 800-993-3690

Grunke's First Street Inn (Bayfield): 715-779-5480 or
800-245-3072

Old Rittenhouse Inn (Bayfield): 715-779-5111

Apostle Islands National Lakeshore Visitor Center (Bayfield):
715-779-3397

Apostle Islands Cruise Service (Bayfield): 715-779-3925 or
800-323-7619

Pier Restaurant (Bayfield): 715-779-3330

Madeline Island Chamber of Commerce (La Pointe):
715-747-2801 or 888-475-3386

Madeline Island Ferry Line (La Pointe): 715-747-2051

Madeline Island Historical Museum (La Pointe): 715-747-2415

Madeline Island Bus Tours (La Pointe): 715-747-2051

Big Bay State Park: 715-747-6425

Lake Superior Big Top Chautauqua (Bayfield): 715-373-5552
  or 888-244-8368

U.S. Forest Service (Washburn): 715-373-2667

Ashland Chamber of Commerce: 715-682-2500 or
  800-284-9484

Ashland Historical Museum: 715-682-4911

Hotel Chequamegon (Ashland): 715-682-9095

Index